PENDO

PENDO

GOD LOVES AFRICA!

Martha Kirkpatrick

Foreword
by
Malon McVey

authorHOUSE®

AuthorHouse™
1663 Liberty Drive
Bloomington, IN 47403
www.authorhouse.com
Phone: 1-800-839-8640

Published by AuthorHouse   07/25/2012

ISBN: 978-1-4772-1567-8 (sc)
ISBN: 978-1-4772-1566-1 (e)

Library of Congress Control Number: 2012910220

Contents

DEDICATION

This book is lovingly dedicated to

the memory of

Elizabeth Faye Kirkpatrick

and

Joel Craig Kirkpatrick.

ACKNOWLEDGEMENTS

I would like to thank Malon McVey for his work in editing this book. It became a much bigger effort than I ever planned because of his questions about everything African and constant urging to reveal more about our life in Africa. Malon and his wife Jennie have been our prayer partners, along with Dr. Miriam Olver, for several years now.

I would also like to thank Courtney Coates for her eager willingness to proofread the results. Courtney has been our lead pastor's wife at Indianapolis First Free Methodist Church for several years. We will miss their family as they move on to further studies.

I could thank my husband Jim, but how do you thank someone you have lived with for fifty-two years. This is really our mutual project, because I don't know where my thoughts end and his begin. We are one and united in our efforts to be our best for the Lord Jesus Christ wherever we are.

Above all, I am thanking our grandson Philip Kendall for his recording my telling, and later his sending as email attachments, the stories contained in this book. Without his push, this book probably would never have happened.

EDITOR'S FOREWORD
By Malon McVey

Martha has chosen the Swahili word, *Pendo,* as the title for this book because it means *Love.* She reminisces about a Swahili song that says, "The love of God is great. We are happy to know that."

Martha loved to hear Africans sing this in special meetings, funerals and weddings.

Since Martha was called to Africa from childhood, God's love for Africa is paramount in her heart.

In English we sing the Frederick M. Lehman song, "The love of God is greater far than tongue or pen can ever tell. It goes beyond the highest star and reaches to the lowest hell."

The term, *pendo*, is a contraction of the word, *upendo*, which has the same meaning. The contraction is used in completing a meter for a song or poem. It is also used as a name.

Central Africans tended to have nicknames for white missionaries. One of the reasons for nicknames was that the white missionaries would not know of whom the Africans were speaking. At the end of her forty-one year missions career in central Africa, Martha discovered her nickname, Pendo.

Chapter 1

Why this book?

Why would I want to write a book? Or tell these stories? Well, it's like this . . .

One time, recently, a friend asked me "Why don't you write a book?" I said "You're the thousandth person to ask me that . . . but I am afraid that nobody would read it if I did write it." She answered, "A thousand people would." So I'm counting on that.

The second reason why I'd write a book is because many relatives of former missionaries have come to me and said "Oh! My grandpa, or my great grandma was a missionary in Africa." I would ask, "Where did your grandparent serve?" They would say, "I don't know . . ." I do not want our grandchildren ever to have to say that. I want them to know where we lived in Africa, what it was like, and what happened to us in Africa, and why we went there. It is part of keeping the story alive.

The third reason is that I regret so much that I never talked to my grandparents about their life before I was born. I don't know if our children talked to my parents about their life before the grandchildren were born. Somehow we have to work hard because we are such a mixed race/mixed races now. We have to be diligent to pass the story on from one generation to another. I feel that is something that God wants us to do. Our children, our grandchildren, and our great grandchildren need to know what their inheritance is. We will never be able to give our children or grandchildren great sums of money. But I do hope and pray that we pass on to them our faith in God and the knowledge that God keeps his promises to our children. That is one of my goals in life.

Philip Kendall, our grandson, (see chapter 15 for the story of his birth.) came from Olympia, WA, and spent a month with us in Indiana the summer of 2010, recording my stories. It was his way of getting this book started, and I am grateful. So the stories in this book were given orally to Philip in the traditional African way. He sent them to me via email this past Christmas. I discovered that my telling a story and writing it are done very differently! There has been lots of revision. Now as the book is finished, I feel deluged with memories of many other good stories that happened in Africa that are not included in this book. So if your story with us is not here, please don't feel bad. The half has not been told of God's faithfulness to us and to the church in central Africa. Especially I think of the faithful International Child Care Ministries workers that spent long hours alone, getting ready for distributions of donations and translating letters to send home to sponsors. The ones who served the longest are Elie Ndaruhutse, Japhet Nsanze, Tuzza, Kaluba Mathias Macinda, and Kay Godoye. I would never have made it without them. I am forever grateful. Also I worked with all the International Child Care Ministries directors: Dr. Alton Gould (the founder), Miss Gertrude Haight, Miss Sylvia Fox (also a missionary colleague), and most recently Mrs. Ann Van Valin. I feel honored to have been a link in the chain with all of them to reach the children in central Africa. All the donors and the workers are part of the reason for the education of pastors' children and orphans in central Africa.

Our children have their own stories which are not mine to tell, but I want everybody who reads this book to know, that one of our greatest witnesses to the Africans, Christians or not, was our children. Many Africans told us they knew we loved them because of how our children treated them.

Whom do I want the book to be for? Other than our grandchildren, I want my thousand friends to have a book to read—the people that love to listen to my stories . . . . These stories describe what God does and has done. That's what I want people to get from the book. Maybe I need to tell more about the exotic and fun things that we did.

There were so many things in Africa that would take your breath away because it was so beautiful, so unusual. I just knew that God put this singular happening here to help *me* carry on; to make *me* happy; to let *me* know that God is present. This happened again and again. My mind flashes through so many things. Here is an example:

We were traveling on New Year's day back to Butare and Kigali in the early 1990's. We were three carloads of people: one from Butare, one from Kigali, and one from Kibogora, and we were traveling in convoy. One of the people was the recently widowed mother of Vernon DeMille, who was a missionary in Kigali. She had been a missionary in Mozambique. She was sad and lonely; it was a big change in her life. We parked in the rainforest to have a picnic lunch and there were 14 great turacos in a tree right beside the road. They stayed there. They are unique, exotic; with red and yellow and green feathers and ugly

3

beaks. They are so shy. They stayed there in that tree right by where we were picnicking the whole time. Besides them, there were monkeys jumping around in the trees. We also saw a mongoose. It's the only time in all our years of going back and forth in that rainforest that we ever saw anything like that. We all felt that this was a gift that God gave to Mrs. DeMille on her way through. She was thrilled. I still think that she did not realize this was a unique happening, as if we saw it every time.

Everywhere we moved, Jim would always build me a birdbath outside the dining room window so that I could watch the birds bathe. African friends did not understand why I would not let the birds bathe in private. In Nairobi we lived in a two story duplex. Jim had the birdbath out there and it was far enough away from the window so that the office that we had right above the dining room looked down on that birdbath too. I looked out that office window one morning and there were those turacos all drinking water out of that birdbath. They were timid and shy but there they were. I went running downstairs as fast as I could so I could take a picture of them—they were gone by the time I got there. I never got the picture, but I surely do have the memory.

What I want everybody to know most of all is that God loves Africa!

Chapter 2

What a Heritage!

Pioneer missionaries have been called "iron men in iron ships." I am glad we served in the era we did, but when I say that, Jim reminds me that we lived through a genocide that lasted over two years and other civil disturbances in Africa that pioneer missionaries did not experience.

Virgil Leroy Kirkpatrick and Faye Elizabeth (Craig) Kirkpatrick, Jim's parents, served God faithfully in Africa for many years. The Kirkpatricks were both from Mansfield OH. They were in the same youth group in a Congregational Church. Their youth director, a business man, went to Camp Sychar, an interdenominational campmeeting at Mt. Vernon, OH. He was saved and sanctified there. Then he took the youth group there and they were saved. When evangelical enthusiasm among the youth became too much for the staid Congregationalists, the Congregational Church expelled the youth director and the youth from the church. They formed a nondenominational church called Pilgrim Church. Years later they joined the Evangelical Friends. When Jim's folks went to Africa, both Camp Sychar and their home church supported them while they were with World Gospel Mission and later with the Africa Revival Fellowship.

Virgil was a missionary for 50 years. Many of Virgil's family and friends called him Kirk and many of his African friends called him *Kaka* (a Kirundi term meaning "the important one"). Fresh out of Asbury Theological Seminary, he went around the world with classmates Byron Crouse and Eugene Erny evangelizing. They formed a trio, both singing and preaching in revivals. Kirk and Faye married in secret just before he left on that round-the-world trip that lasted two and a half years.

Why am I glad I did not serve in Africa in the era of Jim's parents? Kirk and Faye lived in temporary housing (tents and grass-roofed dirt-floored houses) for 25 years, establishing the church wherever they lived. Faye was very afraid of snakes. Their first night in a burned-brick house with a tile roof, concrete floor and screens in the windows, Faye sat on the floor in the living room and cried. She was happy and felt secure. In the morning when she went to the new kitchen to make breakfast, she found many little black mambas on the floor. (Black mambas are one of the most venomous snakes in the world. Mature black mambas average close to 10 feet in length. They are also the fastest snakes in the world and can move 10-12 miles per hour. They can and have chased down full-grown men and killed them.) Apparently a black mamba climbed into the roof structure and laid eggs while the house was being built. The baby snakes had fallen from an access opening in the ceiling which was put there for storage. African friends got the snakes out in a hurry, but Faye always said that God let that happen to remind her that her security was in Him, not in a nice house!

Kirk and Faye had five children all born in Africa. The youngest child, Bob, used to say, "Wouldn't it have been awful if one of us would have been born in the States?" The second child, Marilyn Beth was a year old when the little family got on a ship to go around the southern tip of Africa and on home to Ohio for their first furlough (the modern term is "home assignment"). The little one became ill with a kidney infection while on board. The family short-landed—disembarked before their planned destination—in Port Elizabeth, South Africa. Marilyn was admitted to the hospital, where she died. Consider the grief of Don the oldest child, the parents as they continued their journey, and the folks at home who expected to see a one-year old who had instead been buried in South Africa. Kirk had "Marilyn Dawn" carved on her headstone when he returned to South Africa years later. The next child born was Jim. Faye had hoped for another daughter, but was blessed with four sons. Marilyn was a treasure laid up in heaven. The parents' testimony of victory through loss resulted in several young Bible college students offering their lives to serve as missionaries.

It should be noted that in all her years in Africa Faye suffered from an enlarged heart. Much of the time they lived at altitudes of 6000 feet, yet she accomplished so much. Nowadays she would have been disqualified to serve as a missionary.

* * *

Faye did not finish at Asbury College. She got typhoid fever while in college and used all her money trying to get well. When Kirk started his world tour, he left Faye teaching in Methodist Mountain Missions school in Whitesburg,

Kentucky. She had been teaching there while Kirk was in seminary and continued the next year. Then she got word that her teenage brother had bone cancer. Faye left teaching to care for her brother. He died a year later. The morning after he died, Faye testified that she heard the voice of Jesus saying, "Behold, I come quickly . . . Watch and pray." Whether it was really a voice as she said it was, or it was simply in her mind, she often shared this message. It was a pivotal experience for Faye, and she often talked about it when she gave her testimony.

Kirk was an amazing man! In his first 25 years in Africa, while he was busy directing and teaching in a Bible school for training pastors, he also directed a building program. He would have as many as 300 people on the payroll that would be doing everything from making bricks to building. Always he was active in planting the church in new areas. I regret I could not know him then, but if the word of African Christians means anything, his efforts in revival, teaching, and having a Christ-like spirit were a wonderful influence in building the strong church that exists in central Africa today. Besides all else he did, his correspondence with prayer partners in the United States was of great importance to him.

Many Africans would tell us in our post-colonial era that Jim's dad was the first white man they ever saw. In the last half of his career in Africa, Kirk had a big tent that he would take out on the hills of Burundi, Rwanda, and Congo to hold meetings. Mornings he taught training seminars for pastors; afternoons the pastors evangelized in the surrounding villages, and evenings Kirk and others preached to those same villagers in the big tent. He also showed films to present the gospel to lay people. The electrical power source was a gasoline generator. Kirk would haul barrels of gas in the back of his pickup, using the fuel for both his pickup and the generator. Kirk used a Bell and Howell 16 millimeter movie projector to show the films. He had an Ansco slide projector, a simple PA system with two all-weather horns and a few lights strung around the big tent. He made some of his own films using a Bolex movie camera. Many were saved in those meetings. Kirk had a little tent that he slept in.

Kirk was aided in his travels by Philip Runyenyeri, an African national from Kayero in eastern Burundi. He witnessed as a teenager that God called him to travel with Kirk and care for him. He was a man of very small stature. He lived with the family at Mweya, the station where the Bible Institute was located. Part of the time there was another worker named Philip, who was from Mweya where Kirk made his headquarters when he wasn't traveling. Their duties were to do laundry by hand and iron the laundry with a flatiron heated on the wood stove. They also cooked the family's meals and mended Kirk's tents. In camp they cooked over an open fire. They would cook partridge that Kirk had hunted, as well as rice and greens. Kirk carried dried fruit with him. He would buy pineapple and avocados from the local Africans. Kirk would often eat raw oatmeal for the evening meal with powdered milk that had been mixed with water. The food was tasty. I enjoyed going to visit Kirk out on the hills in the meetings he held when we got there. Most of the time, it was Philip Runyenyeri who traveled with Kirk as his personal assistant. He was faithful and honest. He later married and had a family.

Faye had no medical training, but she treated sick people in the backyard of their home for years. She got her medical education from a tropical medicine handbook. When Jim was home from boarding school, he would help her. She had a special concoction, a German recipe, called black salve (a mixture of sulfur and black and red lead) which she would melt on the stove and then apply to an infected ulcer on the skin after she cleaned it out well with Dettol (a British antiseptic). We still used black salve till it was stolen in the war of 1994 along with the rest of our belongings. I had the recipe but never made any. The recipe was stolen too. Her black salve worked every time. She would tell us of one woman with a very infected sore on her leg that she was treating. A doctor came and saw the sore and took her to be cared for. The woman died. Faye felt that if the patient had been left to her, the woman would have lived. She treated parasites by passing out buckets of epsom salts. She also treated malaria with quinine. There were no clinics in the primitive area where they lived and were establishing the church. Faye's happiest days were at Mweya where she loved and cared for the homesick missionary children living in a dormitory and teaching English in the Bible Institute.

Sometimes Faye went with Kirk as he traveled. Once they went to Baraka, Congo, where they slept in a vacant house that missionaries of another group had left behind. It is hot at Baraka all the time. Baraka is at 2500 feet elevation, the same as Bujumbura, Burundi. Both are right on Lake Tanganyika. Since they are so near the equator, temperatures often stayed around 90 degrees Fahrenheit. Kirk and Faye left the door open with only a screen door between them and the great outdoors. One morning when they got up, they discovered the screen split and all of Faye's clothes stolen. For the rest of that trip she wore one of Kirk's shirts and a sheet for a wraparound skirt.

Tea time was important to Faye, so when they traveled, she carried her thermos of hot tea already prepared. Tea time was a way of keeping hydrated as well as a rest break. On one of those trips, when they got to the border in those post-colonial times, officials did not deal kindly with Philip the assistant. They beat him. This was post-colonial times and the Congolese did not like black Africans devoted to working for a white family. Faye stood between Philip and the government official and said, "You don't touch him without dealing with me first." The government official then proceeded to search their belongings in the car. He stuck his finger in the thermos of tea. Faye took it from him and poured it out on the ground in front of him. This was after independence from Belgium had been proclaimed and pioneer missionaries often found it difficult to cooperate with young, inexperienced political leaders who were trying to find their way.

The first 25 years of their missionary career Kirk and Faye were with the National Holiness Missionary Society, which later became World Gospel Mission (WGM), Marion, IN. The rest of the time Kirk founded an independent board called Africa Revival Fellowship (ARF). The board consisted of friends, many of them Methodists from eastern Pennsylvania and New Jersey who had supported him in his early days as an evangelist. Kirk reported to them regularly. Their main function was fund-raising.

Jim's parents served first in Kenya, Africa. Kirk bought a farm near Kericho at a place called Cyagayik. He intended to build the school for training pastors there. He wanted to buy property in a city but settled for more economical property in the countryside. However, Brooke Bond Tea Company from England offered him such a good a price for it that he sold the farm. Marilyn and Jim were born where the tea factory now stands. The hillsides are covered with tea bushes. It is gorgeous. The best tea in Kenya is produced there. Now it's called the Kenya Tea Packers. The tea is called KETEPA Tea. Kirk then bought land in the city of Kericho where

Kenya Highlands Bible College now stands. World Gospel Mission built the buildings on campus.

When the family moved to Burundi after one term in Kenya, Kirk later was able to build student housing and a duplex at Mweya with proceeds from the tea farm sale. There was still money left over to buy a new 1954 Ford when the family went on home assignment. Jim took his driving test for his U. S. driver's license in that vehicle. Kirk wore out the 1954 Ford in the US. He bought a Chevrolet Carry All (prehistoric SUV) to take to Africa. The Carry All took at least two months to make the voyage.

Later when they went back to Africa from home assignment in the U.S., they moved into an apartment next door to Gerald and Marlene Bates, new Free Methodist missionaries at Ngagara in Bujumbura, Burundi. Gerald is now a retired bishop of the Free Methodist Church. Faye would often have Gerald and Marlene over for a cup of tea or a meal. Gerald later told us that he was never sure what was in Faye's salad. He was sure she went outside; picked the first weed she found and put it in the salad.

In 1963 Kirk bought an Airstream trailer and shipped it to Africa. The trailer was to go with the big tent when he held meetings on the hillsides. This was to make it easier for Faye to live in Africa. Previously, during travel, Faye had to live in a tent and sleep on a cot. In the Airstream, Faye had a dwelling, a refrigerator, a range, a good bed and maybe most importantly—screened windows and a door. When Kirk later established his base on Mweya hill, he also built a shelter for the Airstream along with an office and a shelter for another old camper he had taken to Africa in 1937. The old camper they used for visitors. It was positioned right beside the beautiful home that Kirk and his oldest son Don had built in the center of Mweya, also named Windy Hill, situated in the mountains of central Burundi. He had a Ford pickup he used to pull the trailer.

Mweya was probably the biggest mission station in Burundi. In that day missions propagated through "mission stations" or compounds in which missionaries lived in groups. Mweya was a Free Methodist mission station but it was too close to a nearby Friends center to have a mission station. The Free Methodists offered Mweya as a cooperative site to work with the Friends and World Gospel Mission as well as Free Methodists. The mission station housed the missionary children's school, a cooperative printing establishment, Mweya Bible Institute for training pastors, as well as homes for personnel, dormitories, and the Free Methodist Church. The whole station was operated by a board of appointed missionaries from the World Gospel Mission, Free Methodist Mission and Evangelical Friends Church.

As long as Kirk was there, he was the heart and center of Mweya. Not much happened without his blessing. As mentioned, he and his oldest son Don built the big house in the center of the station. He also built the first Bible school buildings and the main section of the printing establishment. We lived in the big house during our four years at Mweya. Mweya is at 5800 feet elevation. It has been struck several times by lightning. Once, lightning struck when the U.S. ambassador and his wife were having lunch at our house. We had an African worker named Simeon. The ambassador took off for the kitchen, because he thought Simeon might have been struck if he had his hands in the dish water. How many missionaries have had a U.S. ambassador in their kitchen?

Everywhere Kirk went he took trees to plant. Some were fruit trees such as orange, lemon, guava, loquats, custard apples, peaches, papaya. Avocado trees were planted on nearly every station. The first avocado trees took ten years to grow till they produced fruit, but later trees produced much more quickly. Other trees produced leaves that made good mulch and lumber for building, such as grevilia (silver maple), cyprus, eucalyptus (flowering and commercial), black wattle (a kind of acacia), and different kinds of pine. The tree seedlings came from colonial Belgian experimental farms, which were continued by African nationals after independence. Sometimes the seedlings were provided fee *gratis*. Other times the seedlings were at very low cost. The fruit trees have generally not been maintained but the other trees flourish to this day. Someone at Mweya asked the elderly Kirk why he would plant trees, since he would never live to eat the fruit or enjoy the shade. Kirk replied that he planted them for the next generation.

No fences were around any house as long as Kirk made his headquarters at Mweya. Everybody among the Africans in our part of Africa had fences around their houses to keep out thieves. The paths to their houses were often crooked, because they believed evil spirits could only follow a straight line. Having no fences was an effort to show trust between Africans and missionaries that lived on the mission station.

It was difficult for children to understand that ripening fruit on trees was out of bounds since the trees were so easily accessible. More than one child was disciplined for getting fruit without permission. Today adults who were children then seem to remember guava fruit fights.

Kirk and Faye spoke mostly Swahili, the first African language they learned in Kenya. They later learned the language of Burundi, Kirundi, but often mixed it with Swahili.

In 1979 the four sons made Kirk return to the United States so they could help him and their mother Faye celebrate their 50th wedding anniversary. Kirk and Faye agreed that for half their married life they were separated because Faye often came to the U.S. for health reasons or to care for relatives. In 1969 Faye retired permanently, while Kirk continued his teaching and evangelizing for another ten years.

In the first 25 years of his missionary career, Kirk helped start the WGM work in Kenya and established mission stations in Burundi at Kayero, Murore, Murehe, and Mweya. He planted and helped build some 40 or 50 churches as well as at least two Bible colleges. The last 25 years of his missionary career, Kirk concentrated on traveling evangelism with his big tent, and on teaching pastors when at home at Mweya. Throughout his missionary career, he was always a strong proponent of Wesleyan holiness.

Faye preceded Kirk in death on her 80th birthday on July 4, 1984. Kirk went to heaven on August 24, 1994, just days before his 94th birthday. They are buried in Mansfield, Ohio.

Grandma Faye beside their Airstream trailer at Mweya

Four generations: Kirk, Len, Jim with Joel in front

Grandma Faye and our
children celebrating Len's first
birthday at Mweya

Faye and Kirk with Len
at Kayero Falls

Chapter 3

Who am I?

My mother Alice Arnett was born near Salyersville, Magoffin County, Kentucky on January 19, 1913. When she was ten years old, the family left at 2 a.m. on the train for Ohio. Alice was the oldest of 12 children. My mother attended the Oak Grove Church of the Brethren. She and my father Oscar Fruth met at a youth gathering in Fostoria, Ohio, Church of the Brethren where my father was a member. Their homes were about ten miles apart. My father was born February 9, 1913. Both of my parents graduated from high school. They were married February 25, 1934.

I cannot recall at all how my grandparents Arnett made a living. I know that by the time I came along my uncle worked at what we called the "muck plant" where they used the black soil to make fertilizer. The muck was just down the road from where my grandparents lived. That uncle never married. He lived at home with his parents.

My mother walked across the field in Ohio to a one room country school house (which was just down the road from where we later lived) through eighth grade. By the time we moved there, the school house had become a chicken house. Mom graduated from high school in Vanlue where her children all went. My grandfather took my two youngest aunts to our country church during revival meetings, but my grandmother never darkened a church door. The coffee pot was always full and hot on the wood stove. Grandma Arnett was often teased for her crooked rows in the garden in the back yard, but she always had a garden. My grandparents Arnett had neither electricity nor running water in the home. They lived across the field from our house from the time I was in first grade.

My grandfather Charles Fruth died in May before I was born in August, so I never knew him. Grandpa had three children by another wife who died when the third child was born. He looked for someone to care for the new infant and found a widow, Eva Schubert Cramer, whose first husband had been a Church of the Brethren pastor. Eva and Ed Cramer had one adopted son. Eva worked out so well in caring for the infant that Charles married her. Charles and Eva then had two sons who were my father Oscar and another son named Schubert. Grandma told me that my father was so small when he was born that he lay in a cigar box which she kept wrapped and near the stove to keep him warm. She said he weighed 2 1/2 pounds. Six children grew up together: his three, her one, and their two.

My father always regretted that he and his siblings let his mother and my grandmother Eva Fruth stay on the farm after her husband died. She died of a stroke at age 72 during my first year at Kentucky Mountain Bible Institute. My father felt that the responsibility was too much for her. Grandma moved into the little house right beside the bigger house where she had lived. Whoever was renting the farm lived in the big house. Grandma chopped her own wood for her kitchen and living room stoves. She had a beautiful garden with fragrant flowers. I felt like her garden was a place out of a story book. She bore the responsibility of renting out the farm. Eventually my father and his first cousin owned the home farm together. They continued to rent out the house. It was 120 acres. 40 acres of that 120 were across the road, and that was the first place my parents lived after they were married. My dad also rented another farm across the road from his home place. Those farms were near Fostoria, Ohio. My father graduated from high school in Fostoria.

I am the eldest of eight children. I was born in a large farm home that belonged to my great grandfather William Schubert (my father's grandfather). He was blind. When we would go to visit my grandmother, he would be there and would want to feel our faces to see if he could guess which one it was. My Grandma Fruth spoke German fluently and knew poems in German. She would quote them to us when she came to visit.

My parents bought 1/3 of a farm just down the road from my great grandfather's after the second child, Catherine, was born. The third child Barbara was born there. When I was in the first grade, my parents bought the farm where we all grew up. It was in Seneca County on the border with Hancock County. It was 60 acres of fertile soil.

The fourth child was Mary Jane. She was born blind on February 14, 1945. My mother had measles when she was three months pregnant with Mary Jane. This was considered the cause of Mary Jane's cataracts. I remember Mom and Dad taking Mary Jane to the doctor when she was still very young. They came home and had us three girls sit down in the living room with them where they told us that Mary Jane was blind. Of course, Mom cried when she told us. After three surgeries on her eyes, Mary Jane died of acute

Bright's disease, a kidney infection, on March 13, 1949, when she was four years old. My recollection is that the Bright's disease was caused by an overdose of anesthetic.

After my blind sister, Mary Jane, started to walk, we never went anywhere as a family till she died. Someone always stayed home with Mary Jane, because she could not be controlled. I wonder if she was deaf. She never learned to talk even though she was four years old when she died. She had a certain sound she made when she wanted a drink of water. She and I shared a bedroom. I loved her dearly and missed her when she died. I was in the sixth grade when she left us.

The next year we welcomed a baby brother named Oscar Fruth. The next year after that we greeted another sister, Beryl. Twenty months later we welcomed identical twin sisters, Rebecca and Rachel. I had already left home to study at Mt. Carmel when Beryl and the twins were born. Since my husband Jim and I started our relationship when the twins were two, they do not remember me without him.

When I was in first grade, my mother's brother, Ed, came to live with us. He helped on the farm and stayed with us from his eighth to 12th grade. I don't know why Ed came to live with us. At the time, I thought it was to help my parents on the farm. It may have been a different reason.

Dad raised wheat, corn, soybeans, alfalfa and clover which were baled for hay. We had a grainery where oats were stored and cribs for the corn, which Dad would take to the elevators at Alvada or Vanlue to have ground for feed for the cows and the pigs. Wheat and soybeans were cash crops. We had sour cherry, pear and apple trees in our yard.

Each spring Mom and Dad would buy 400 baby chickens. Mom would usually fry chicken early in the morning on

Sunday to be ready for dinner after we came home from church. After the younger children came along, Mom always made sure there were four chicken legs so each child could have one. She always said she preferred the neck, but it was really her way of giving the best to Dad and us children. The hens would be sold or butchered and eaten before the young hens came along.

We also raised pigs. When the baby pigs were born while it was still cold in the spring, I remember coming home from school and finding a wooden crate on the register in the dining room with straw in the bottom of the crate and baby pigs nestled in the straw. I hated the smell of the pigs. But they brought in money when they were sold.

Mom and Dad had a big and wonderful garden. We helped as we got older. We got paid five cents for a small basket of strawberries we picked and ten cents a row for hoeing the weeds out of the corn that the cultivator did not get. My mother would take eggs from our hens to the local grocery store five miles away in Vanlue and trade them for what she needed, like coffee, spices, sugar, flour, baking powder, yeast.

From my sixth grade on for some years, Dad hauled farmers' milk to the dairy. That meant he and I got up at 4:30 a.m. He would leave with the truck to pick up other farmers' milk. He would pass by our place at 7:30 to pick up ours, so I would have our seven or eight cows milked and the milk in the cans ready to go. We also milked in the evening. Every cow had a name. One cow named Susie always had to have "kickers" like hand cuffs on her back legs to prevent her from kicking the bucket. I can't remember how many gallons each cow gave. A bucket full was considered a good amount per cow. We kept milk for ourselves and sold the rest. We drank whole milk. When our neighbor got a disease, undulant fever, from the milk, my folks bought a pasteurizer and started pasteurizing. I hated the cream and the "skin" on top of pasteurized milk.

In the spring and summer we would work in the fields, preparing the ground, planting, harvesting. Sometimes I would put the bales on the gasoline-motor-powered elevator and Dad would arrange them in the hay mow. I loved going with Dad up to his farms at his home place to work. It meant driving the tractors along the highway, maybe ten miles away from home. It also meant lunch with Grandma. I have one unpleasant memory of getting the harrow caught in an old fence as I was "working" ground. My dad was not happy, and I can still hear his words, "I have a notion to let you sit here for the rest of the day!" I loved the farm. If I hadn't married a missionary, I hope I would have found a farmer.

When I was in the second grade, a Wesleyan Methodist evangelist named William Wright came to hold a revival meeting at our church. Many farmers started to follow God at that time. We started going to a Friday night cottage prayer meeting. By that I mean it was held in a different farm home each Friday evening. There would be as many as 70 people gathered together. Like most things in the church go, sad to say, people did not always agree. One man started another prayer meeting on Thursday nights. My great uncle, Grandma Fruth's brother named Sam Schubert, had a prayer meeting in his home on Wednesday nights for his children and grandchildren. Uncle Sam and Aunt Dorothy lived down the road from us. He invited and included us. I liked going there because Great Aunt Dorothy would give the kids candy afterwards if we were "good" during Bible study and prayers. We went to all three prayer meetings every week except during harvest. I remember people would say to Dad that he needed to take sides, that they didn't know whose side he was on. I remember his answer, "I'm not on anybody's side. I'm trying to be on God's side!" I have lived by that word all my life.

Our house was heated by a wood stove in the dining room until sometime after Mary Jane was born, because I remember coming downstairs in the morning and finding a bassinet beside the wood stove with a baby in it! School was closed for weeks because of the snow that winter of 1945. The snow was so high and so frozen that we walked on top of the snow that covered the fences all the way to Arnetts' house.

My parents always took us to Sunday school and church in the Oak Grove Church of the Brethren. Dad taught us what to say when we prayed before we went to bed. Both my parents were faithful and devout.

The kitchen and dining room of our house had been a log cabin. Harry Thomas, the former owner of the farm, had moved the cabin down the road a bit and added on the living room and a bedroom downstairs and two bedrooms upstairs. The floor in the dining room and kitchen were not as level and strong-feeling as the other rooms. We had a cellar where the furnace was installed, the washing machine was located, and canned foods that my mother prepared every summer were stored.

Mom was strict about getting the laundry on the line early in the morning. It was a neighborhood reputation thing, it seemed to me. It was important to hang sheets and towels on the line near the road. The rest of the clothes were hung in the back yard. Mom taught us how to hang clothes properly.

I remember before I started elementary school when we bought our first bread from the grocery store. Mom gave my sister and me a loaf and let us eat as much as we wanted. We thought it was delicious.

We went to Findlay Ohio Byal Park Campmeeting every year in August for 10 days. It was 12 miles from the farm and located right beside the Cooper Tire Company on the south side of Findlay, Ohio. The people from Mt. Carmel High School who taught the youth and children stayed in the dormitory. There was also a dining hall. If we ever went in the morning to stay all day, like on missionary day or Sunday, Mom packed our dinner and we ate standing at the trunk of the car.

We worshiped in the tabernacle at camp. It had doors all around the sides with the hinges on the tops of the doors. Each door had a long pole to prop the door open when it was hot. The first years I can remember, there was saw dust on the floor. At some point they cemented the floor.

Hand-held fans were always available from a funeral home.with their advertisement on them. No air conditioning. The camp had morning, afternoon and evening services. Most days, except for the two Sundays and Missionary Day, we arrived in time for the silent prayer bell at 1 p.m. and children's meeting at 1:30. On Sundays and Missionary Day, we went to camp all day. In my growing-up days the tabernacle was full. Attendance dwindled in later years. Finally they sold the camp.

My mother remembered it better than I did. I was five years old. The summer was hot. That year when I was age five was different. When we went home, Mom and Dad sat on the back steps of the farm house and rehashed the afternoon preaching. I remember telling them that I had become a Christian that day and when I grew up, I would be a missionary in Africa. My mother cried and said, "If that is what God wants, then that is what we want." Miss

Genelle Day, a teacher from Mt. Carmel High School, was our teacher in the children's meeting. She asked those who wanted to be saved to come forward and kneel at a bench in the front. Jane Thomas from our home church, who was attending Kentucky Mountain Bible Institute (KMBI, later Kentucky Mountain Bible College) prayed with me. I don't remember feeling guilty; I just remember wanting to belong to Jesus. I was happy and felt close to God.

The first prayer I remember God answering was for a piano. The Evangelical Church beside the cemetery where my family members are buried was to be torn down. As a child I went to that church with my parents for revival meetings. I remember hearing Dr. Warren McIntire preach there. There were no electric lights, just gas lights inside the church. When the auction was held for the furniture inside the church, I was old enough to stay at home alone. All the time my parents were gone I prayed and prayed that God would tell them to buy the piano. When Dad walked into the house, he scratched his head like he did when he was thinking, and he said to my mother, "I don't know what got into me. I had no plan to buy anything there today." I'll never forget how happy I was that God had answered my prayer. We took lessons on it and by the time I went away to high school, I had finished John Thompson's Grade Four. I did my best and music was a comfort but I never won any prizes for my playing.

I loved the farm but always felt I would never stay there for long. Between ten and 12 years of age, I started praying every night before I went to bed that my parents would consider me grown up enough to go to Mt. Carmel High School in southeastern Kentucky. It was 300 miles away from home in the mountains. I had never been there, but every year the founder Dr. Lela G. McConnell would come

25

with a quartet to speak on Missionary Day at Byal Park Campmeeting. Workers from the school would also come to our farm community to get a truckload of food harvested from the gardens and fields once each year. My grandmother Arnett was very much against my going to Mt. Carmel—as were others in the family. They said I would be weird and would starve to death. I considered going to Mt Carmel High School the first step in preparation to go to Africa.

When people in my home church tried to keep me from going to Mt. Carmel, they even accused my parents of abdicating their responsibility of rearing me to a school. My dad took me to visit my great uncle Sam Schubert and asked him what to do. Uncle Sam's oldest child had said she was called to be a missionary but she married quickly and seemed unhappy in her marriage. Her parents must have felt they prevented her from being a missionary. Uncle Sam's answer was, "If God has called Martha to be a missionary, don't put a straw in her way. If you do, you'll have all your life to regret it."

The Kentucky Mountain Holiness Association (KMHA) was founded by Dr. Lela G. McConnell, a graduate of Asbury College (now Asbury University), who felt called to take the gospel to the people in the hills of Appalachia. She took some friends with her from Asbury and others joined her to found Mt. Carmel High School in 1925. Mr. Raymond Swauger was the designer and builder of all the buildings in what was to become the KMHA. He also built a series of bridges spanning the north fork of the Kentucky River at the foot of the hill on which Mt Carmel campus stands. Miss McConnell meant for Mt. Carmel to reach the mountain children. When I was there, some Appalachian children still came to the school. As Miss McConnell traveled to raise awareness of the school and solicit help, young people from other states came to Mt. Carmel. There was not the abundance of Christian day schools we have today. If parents wanted their children educated in a conservative holiness environment, Mt. Carmel was an option. Kentucky Mountain Bible Institute, which later became Kentucky Mountain Bible College, was initially founded in 1932 some four miles away from the high school in an abandoned coal company commissary on Frozen Creek. A flashflood obliterated the campus in 1939. Mrs. Nettie Myers was our dean of women when I was a student at KMBI. She was a widow who lost her husband and three children in that flood. She maintained a room in the women's dormitory. For years, the students heard Mrs. Myers weeping through the nights for her lost family.

Going to Mt. Carmel was not much of an adjustment at all for me. I was focused on getting ready to be a missionary and I wanted to learn how. I was homesick at first when I went there as a freshman, but I loved the school. My first roommates were Ruthan Fisher and Ida Bell Ogg from my Ohio Christian farm community. We lived in the attic of the dormitory in the administration building and the bathroom was in the basement. My favorite subjects were Latin, physics, typing, and piano. I felt secure in the mountains. I loved spring with the dogwoods blooming. I loved walks in the hills when we went on Saturday.

Mr. Swauger stretched a cable with a cable car across the Kentucky River to carry heavy luggage and supplies. The cable car was powered by a car engine. It was not possible to drive to Mt. Carmel until 1957 when Mr. Swauger built the low water bridge across the north fork of the Kentucky River. Roads were available but they circled around through Jackson. Miss McConnell chose the back side of the north fork of the Kentucky River. Children back in the hills could

27

get a grade school education in the small community grade schools but could not get to the county seat, Jackson, to attend high school. In 1986 the Martha Layne Collins Bridge was built over the same site as Mr. Swauger's low water bridge. The state highway engineers were sure they could take out the low water bridge in a couple days. They spent several days trying to dig out the bridge. They then spent several more days trying to blast out the bridge. The pylons of Mr. Swauger's bridge still stand in the north fork of the Kentucky River. My husband Jim helped pour that low water bridge during the summer work program.

At Mt. Carmel I earned ten cents an hour working on campus. I worked in the darkroom with Rev. Henrietta News and a couple other students, Betty Small and Ruth Davis Cundiff. We produced the pictures for the annual, took family pictures and class pictures. I also worked on a cooking crew in the kitchen. We had two crews and took turns preparing breakfast and the evening meal. Ruth Davis Cundiff and I made the morning biscuits. We were always trying to make ours fluffier than the other morning team. Miss Alice Spatz, the campus cook, advised me not to overdo the baking powder. I also worked with Agnes Creed Neihof washing windows. Ruth and Robert Cundiff and Agnes and Dr. Eldon Neihof remain our close friends to this day. My junior and senior years I supervised the evening study hall. My husband, Jim, remembers those study halls. Our school week was Tuesday through Saturday. We followed this unusual weekly schedule so that we students could have an evening study hall before every school day. Our laundry was done communally and we had to gather our own clothes off the line when they were dry. We were allowed two showers a week, five minutes each. Mr. Swauger designed and built the water supply system for a much smaller campus population. Conservation was strictly enforced.

Increasingly though, I felt that if I were going to be a missionary, I surely needed more of God than I had. I went home to work on the farm the summer after my freshman year. The local Oak Grove Church of the Brethren, where my parents were members, had a revival meeting that June. It was special because people got saved and sanctified who had been without a witness before. They came from other churches to the meeting. The special speaker was Edith Lockard from the Kentucky Mountain Holiness Association. The musician was Elma Reed, the music teacher for years at Mt. Carmel High School. I went forward to pray after every message preached that week. I confessed, surrendered and pleaded with God to make me holy. Dad had me take the week off from work on the farm so I could pray.

Finally, the last Sunday when we pulled into the drive at home after church, Dad asked me to stay behind in the car when the rest of the family went into the house. He told me the choice was up to me. I could spend the rest of my life struggling or I could accept by faith in God that He had done what He said He would do if we confess and surrender all. I did that then and there and felt at rest. That evening in the closing service at the church I went forward and publicly announced that I now belonged completely to God. Life was different after that!

I have often wondered how different life could have ended for me and other youth in the community if the Church of the Brethren had pursued our becoming members. I think no one ever invited us to be members. Their love feasts and communion services were closed sessions, so I never witnessed one. I only heard my parents talk about it. I know that that they practiced foot washing in those closed sessions.

My sister next to me, Catherine, was often frail and sick. Dad bought special vitamins called Plenamins for her. She had her tonsils out during high school vacation. I can't remember if it was Christmas or spring vacation. We were roommates that year at Mt. Carmel High School. She was a freshman, and I was a junior. Our first night back at school she had a horrible sulfa reaction. Sulfa was the precursor to penicillin, a wonder drug for treating infections. However, sulfa allergies are common. I stayed up all night with her, as did Miss Vandewarker. "Miss Vande" was the nurse at Mt. Carmel then. I was so afraid Catherine was going to die. She seemed healthier after that. She and my sister Beryl were the most intelligent in our family, in my estimation. My brother Oscar would tell people that he was the dumb one in the family. He graduated third in his class.

During Mt. Carmel days there were 45 students in my class and real competition. Paul Good, son of Dr. Harold Good, then secretary of World Gospel Mission, was the tallest in our class, and I was the shortest. We finished four years at Mt. Carmel with a small difference in our grade average. Paul won. He apologized to me after graduation and said I should have been valedictorian instead of him.

My friend and classmate Ruthan Fisher and I received letters from the same fellow, a classmate, the summer after we graduated. When my parents found out we were both receiving letters from the same person, they would not let me write to him. They said that was like two-timing and I shouldn't participate. Later he promised to come and visit Ruthan on a certain day. She got all ready for the visit and waited and waited. He never showed up. When I heard that, I was glad I did what my folks said to do.

It seemed to me that the natural thing for a prospective missionary going to Mt. Carmel was to go to Kentucky Mountain Bible Institute after graduating from high school. We earned 25 cents an hour working on campus. I worked in the registrar's office with Mrs. Alice Fisher. I typed official transcripts of students' records to send when they applied for further training. There could not be a single mistake on a transcript—no erasures, no correction fluid. There was no electric typewriter. Computers had not shown up yet! Because the registrar's office was not considered "hard" work, I worked in Miss Archer's flower gardens after the evening meal. I also sat in the office during the evening study halls and received calls from the outside for faculty or students. I had to hunt down the person called and get them to the phone as fast as I could. We followed the same weekly school schedule as Mt Carmel. Mondays we did not have classes so that people could rest from travels to churches in the hills. I traveled to those churches on Sunday but I also cleaned the big stoves in the kitchen some Mondays and butchered chickens other Mondays. I worked with Agnes Creed Neihof butchering chickens. Jim Kirkpatrick caught and killed the chickens.

My favorite classes at KMBI were Greek and Old Testament prophets. I think the speech class taught by Rev. Henrietta Griffith was the most helpful class for me. The summer between my junior and senior year I stayed at school and worked in the office to prepare a book so one could see at a glance the point standing instead of having to figure it every time. During that summer Mrs. Fisher and I had to take turns working in the office and the kitchen, because some felt the office work was not as strenuous as the kitchen work. That summer I also drove Miss Archer to meetings out in KMHA churches and would stay there for the duration of the revival meeting.

I remember that during my first year at KMBI, Jim's parents came to visit. Jim and his parents and brothers sang special songs for us in the dining hall after dinner. I was so impressed by their testimony and singing of "I Know Who Holds Tomorrow" that I cried and cried. Little did I know then how I would be tied to that family for life.

I had spent all day one Monday butchering chickens and my autobiography was due the next day for English Composition. It was after Christmas my freshman year at KMBI. I was tired and felt dirty and was sitting on my bed writing when my roommate Agnes Creed Neihof came to tell me that Jim Kirkpatrick wanted to see me down in the music practice room. She gave me a pretty hanky to carry and put some perfume on my neck and away I went. I was so excited when he asked me for a date (my first) that I could not eat for a week. No dates were allowed in the high school. We could talk at the dining room tables with the boys but we were not to single one out for a conversation or meet anywhere on campus. At KMBI the fellow had to get permission from the dean of women, Nettie Myers, to ask a girl for a date. No one could date until the second semester of their freshman year. The girl also had to be interviewed by the dean of women and pray about it before she accepted the proposed date. Forget about trying to date someone if the two of you testified to different evangelistic calls. Going through all that, nobody had just one date! Friday night was dress-up-for-dinner and date night. The fellow would sit with the girl at the table she was assigned. A parlor in the administration building had sofas where couples could sit to visit on date night. Promptly at 9 p.m., date night was over. Soon after our first date I got a call from Miss Genelle

Day to visit her at Mt. Carmel. She informed me that she thought there was no one at KMBI for me to marry. Then my dad came to visit, probably when someone from the home community brought a load of produce to the school. I was so excited to have him meet Jim that I introduced Jim before greeting Dad myself. Dad let me know I had not yet greeted him. When Dad and I had time alone, I told Dad what Miss Day had said. He said that I was not to think of marrying anybody yet, but to get to know people and see which one I liked best. So I decided on getting to know Jim. Jim was a year ahead of me in school and when he finished his three years at KMBC, he went to Asbury College (now university) to get a bachelor's degree.

Both Asbury and Marion transferred credit hours from KMBI for courses they also offered, so Jim graduated from Asbury College two years later. I took three years to graduate, because Mom and Dad wanted me to meet teaching requirements. They insisted that I be able to support myself if anything happened to my husband. I never taught in U.S. schools, but I was always teaching wherever we lived in Africa.

My senior year at KMBI I dated another fellow, who said he was called to Africa. In our KMBI graduating class we were 21 students: 14 girls and seven fellows. Two girls for every fellow! We both applied to Marion College and went there. I had a job at World Gospel Mission as secretary in the Prayer Band Department. I lived with a widow who worked in the WGM Bookstore and went to Marion College (now Indiana Wesleyan University—IWU). I was so lonesome! Dad bought me a 1950 Chevrolet coupe for Christmas that year. Until then I had been taking the bus to school and walking to work. In the summers I traveled for the Prayer

Band Department to contact prayer groups of WGM in the interdenominational campmeetings.

Two issues became clear to me in my loneliness at Marion College. One issue was that life in the world was very different from life on the farm as well as at Mt. Carmel and at KMBI. I needed a friend in this world. That is not to say I did not have friends, but it is to say that this was the first time in my life I slept in a room by myself. Secondly, I could think of no one in the world that held a candle to Jim Kirkpatrick. Our backgrounds were very different. I loved everything to do with the farm. Jim knew scarcely anything about farming in the U.S. He had an ear for music which I do not have. He was far ahead of me in knowledge of other cultures and languages, but I knew I could learn. Everybody who knows us knows we are opposites, but opposites attract. I loved Jim for his gentleness and courtesy. I knew he would be good to me. As Ruth Cundiff Davis advised me, "Jim will never drag you back to America from Africa against your will." All the time I've known Jim, he has always tried to be very sensitive to listen for the leadings of the Lord in our lives. We had one goal in common, which was to make Jesus known to people who needed Him. I was happiest when I was with Jim.

That summer before I started my first year at Marion College whom should I meet in the Sychar Camp near Mt. Vernon Ohio, but Jim Kirkpatrick, who was representing his dad's mission group Africa Revival Fellowship. I felt like I had gone to heaven! I went back to attend Marion College for a year.

Jim found ways to get himself to Marion, Indiana, to visit me. On one of those trips he asked me to marry him! I said I would! I drove myself down to Wilmore, Kentucky, for his graduation from Asbury College. He and his brother Tim had an apartment on North Lexington Street in the French teacher Miss Hayes' house for the next year. I transferred to Asbury College to be near (major in) Jim. I lived in Glide-Crawford Hall with Elizabeth Hinshaw who graduated that year from KMBI in the same class as Tim. I worked in the Registrar's Office with Mrs. Clara Mikkelson for whom Mrs. Alice Fisher had also worked when she was a student at Asbury. Mrs. Fisher is the one who got me that job. The busiest time in a registrar's office is during vacations, so I stayed and worked to clear my bill. I also stayed with Dr. Warren McIntire's wife whenever he went away in revival meetings. Jim worked in maintenance and as a night watchman.

In the spring we planned our wedding for June 24, 1960. It was the first wedding in 40 years in the Oak Grove Church of the Brethren that I attended as a child. We had candles in our wedding. There was an outcry from some of the conservatives over that. "You might as well have had it in a Catholic Church, if you're going to have candles," they said. A neighbor lady, Bernice Van Horn, made our dresses: mine, Catherine's and Barbara's. Her daughter made the wedding cake. Ran and Ellen Boggs from KMHA sang, and my friend from Nelson Street Wesleyan Methodist Church, Merwin Logsdon, played the piano. Her father who was my pastor in Marion and Jim's father performed the wedding ceremony. Tim was best man. I told Tim that he had one responsibility and that was to get Jim to the church on time! I wanted to take the "thee's" and "thou's" out of the wedding ceremony, but Jim's dad made it sound so awkward without them that we left them in.

There was no ring ceremony in our wedding, because the church I grew up in believed that Christians did not wear jewelry. Jim and I went together to a pawn shop in Lexington, Kentucky, and bought a wedding ring that fit me for five dollars. On our way to a motel after the reception Jim pulled the car over to the side of the road and put that ring on me. It was a good one, the one I'm still wearing. For all the time we lived in Wilmore, Kentucky, and Pulaski, Michigan, where we pastored before we went to Africa, I took off the wedding ring when we went home to the farm. Mom and Dad never knew I had one. We stayed with them for awhile before we left for French study in Belgium. One day Dad and I were going somewhere in the car. He surprised me by saying that he had been thinking about it, and he thought Jim should get me a ring to wear in Europe. It was then I told him I had had one since the day we married. Years later we got one for Jim. Mom never did agree with either one of us having one.

In June of 1961, Tim and I graduated from Asbury College. I majored in English in secondary education. We went home to Ohio for my sister Catherine's wedding to Harry Taylor just before graduation. We drove through the night to get back in time for our college graduation. We all three, Tim, Jim and I, overslept and had to rush to get Tim and me in the graduation line. Jim slammed his hand in the door of the car in the rush. I was pregnant and tired and nauseated. It took all the discipline I had to sit through that graduation exercise, but I made it and got that Bachelor of Arts degree.

On October 15, 1961, we welcomed Elizabeth Faye Kirkpatrick into our home. I think Dad never did appreciate that we had a baby before Jim finished seminary. We could ill afford a child, but I always felt that Mom and Dad were poor ones to advise us since they had eight children. We often felt they could not afford us, but they always stood by us and helped us when we needed them.

My Grandma Fruth with my
brother Oscar

Oscar Fruth family

The farm where we grew up

Chapter 4

Jim

Jim was born at Chagayik near Kericho in Kenya. He was the third child of Virgil Leroy and Faye Elizabeth Craig Kirkpatrick. His sister, the second child, died before he was born. Jim's parents named him Virgil Eugene Kirkpatrick. The "Eugene" was for Eugene Erny who had traveled around the world with his father right after their completion of Asbury Seminary. The plan was to nickname Jim "Gene" but the African nursemaid that helped care for Jim pronounced "Gene" as "Zheem" and he became "Jim." Fifteen months later Jim's brother Tim was born. They named him Charles Byron Kirkpatrick, planning to called him Byron. Byron was for Byron Crouse, the other member of the trio that traveled round the world. Charles was for an uncle. The World Gospel Mission American nurse Trudy Shryock who attended the birth said, "Oh, no, it has to be something that rhymes with Jim." She called him Tim. It stuck. All their growing up years they were Jim and Tim, not officially, but everybody knew and knows them as Jim and Tim. When Jim went to Asbury College, he decided he would be known as Virgil, so people who had been there awhile would know that he was the son of Virgil Leroy Kirkpatrick. He continued using that name all through Asbury College and Seminary. When we went to southern Michigan to pastor for two years, he continued with that name. When we meet people and they greet him as Virgil, I always know what era of his life they got to know him in.

Jim was eighteen months old when the family moved to Burundi. The parents waited till Tim was born to make the move. Tim was born at Kaimosi, the main Friends mission station in Kenya. Tim was three months old when they made the move to Burundi.

The family lived first at Kayero, a place in eastern Burundi given to WGM by the Free Methodists to start a mission station. Free Methodists had already built a couple rooms there before Kirkpatricks arrived. The country of Burundi had been divided up among the different Protestant missions so that the whole country would be reached. The Free Methodists felt they had more than they could handle (the Free Methodists were responsible for the "middle" of Burundi, as well as the western and eastern edge). When WGM came, wanting to enter Burundi, the Free Methodists gave them responsibility for the eastern edge. The Kirkpatricks stayed first at Kibuye for six months. Kibuye is the Free Methodist mission station where the mission established a medical center which eventually became a hospital. During that six months, Kirk built an extra room on the house that Colletts had started at Kayero, and then went back to Kenya to bring back more of their things.

There was no road to Kayero, so when it was time for the move from Kibuye to Kayero (30 miles), they drove as far as a ridge across from Kayero called Kamaramagambo. They left the car there and walked to Kayero. Jim thinks it was eight or nine miles. They arrived at night. An African who became their nurse carried Jim and Tim. Jim's mother was not aware that the woman had infectious ringworm in her hair. The nurse always had her head covered. Jim's mom saw her once without her head covering and promptly let her go as a nursemaid. It was too late though. Both Jim and Tim for years had an awful case of ringworm on their heads.

Faye would spend two hours a day pulling infected hairs out of Jim's and Tim's heads. She would put medicine on their heads and then have them wear a leg of a woman's hose made into a stocking cap. Why the stocking caps? They wore the caps for protection, to hold the medicine on their heads, and to hide the infection. For four years Faye battled that ringworm on Jim's and Tim's heads. Jim has horrible memories of that battle.

The family went to Kayero in Burundi in 1940. Ron and Margaret Collett, Free Methodist missionaries, had been at Kayero first for six months and had built the first rooms. When Colletts heard that the Kirkpatricks were going to be at Kayero, they went back to Kibuye. Kirkpatricks and Colletts lived together at Kibuye for six months before the Kirkpatricks' move to Kayero. Margaret Collett loved to tell me stories of their time together when Jim was little.

It is interesting that when Jim and I got to Burundi as appointed missionaries of the Free Methodists, Ron Collett was our mission superintendent as well as the director of the Mweya Bible Institute. He had had a heart attack but was continuing his work. As an observer, I give Ron Collett credit for teaching the African church the importance of keeping statistical records. Every person was important. He trained the African statistical reporter well! Ron Collett taught "make-do" home improvements as well, like coloring whitewash with earth to make pink "paint" for the walls of our home, a mixture of kerosene and beeswax for wax for the concrete floors and for the cars, kerosene in the mop water to kill fleas and ants. They were helpful tips but when paint and wax and insecticide were available at the big Hatton and Cookson store in Bujumbura, that is what I used.

Ron was British (born in England) but was sent to Africa as a Canadian citizen. He was the most exacting, precise person I ever met. Tea time was as important as prayers in their home. His wife Margaret was the best as a cook but she never revealed her recipes. She promised that she would when she got them perfected, but that never happened. I have never tasted a chocolate cake or a lemon meringue pie better than hers. During World War II when gasoline was scarce, Ron would walk with Africans to start or visit new churches. (Margaret would send along a chocolate cake on those trips.)

Bob was born August 22, 1943, at Matana, a British Church Missionary Society hospital. Attending physician was Dr. Len Sharp, also a venerable revivalist and church planter. Jim's mother was ill, continually carrying a roll of toilet paper for tissue and spitting into the tissues. It was decided that it was best for Faye and the children to come home to the States.

They started the trip in early April of 1944. The East African harbors had no regular passenger service because of World War II. The British and Portuguese controlled the ports. Jim's parents decided to go across Africa to get a Portuguese ship from Angola on the west side of Africa. They started out in the family vehicle which was a half ton 1937 Ford pickup. They were four children and two adults. In those days kerosene was sold in five gallon tins. Jim's dad made flat wooden lids for the tops of two of those tins.

Jim's dad still had them when we got out to Africa and gave them to us. We used them for storing small toys. Those tins were put at Faye's feet in the pickup as containers for diapers and food, as well as Jim's and Tim's seats for the trip. Don sat in the center of the seat and Faye held Bob, then seven months old.

They drove 300 miles through Rwanda and up in eastern Congo to Ruwenzore area (Mountains of the Moon), intending to cross the Semiliki River and continue through the Ituri Forest to Stanleyville (now Kisangani). At the Africa Inland Mission Guest House they found out that the ferry that crossed the Semiliki River had been sunk by a big flood. They waited at the Ruwenzore Mission station while Kirk sent African runners to the Heart of Africa Mission (an American interdenominational mission) in the Ituri Forest. A runner is anyone you send with a message and hope to get an answer. A runner could go more cheaply and go where there wasn't a road in this case. A Mr. Williams of the Heart of Africa Mission had a pickup and agreed to come to Semiliki River to pick up the family and take them to Stanleyville. It was 300 miles from the Semiliki River to Stanleyville. Kirk left his pickup at Ruwenzore and came back later to pick it up.

Jim remembers crossing the crocodile-infested river in dugout canoes. It took several trips to get all their baggage across. They began the journey through the forest but Mr. Williams' pickup had electrical problems. They had to stop often for repairs. Jim remembers looking from the back of the pickup and seeing a gorilla come out on the road after they had passed.

The Semiliki River drains Lake Edward and flows into Lake Albert in the Nile system which is different from the Congo River system. They had to cross the Continental

Divide before descending into the Ituri Forest which is drained by the Congo River. At nightfall they crossed a tributary of the Congo River on a pontoon ferry on Jim's sixth birthday. As Williams' pickup came off the ferry and climbed a river bank, Jim remembers a loud backfiring. The engine of that pickup was not in good repair. They lodged that night at a Catholic mission at the top of the bank. Dessert served was rice pudding with raisins in it. Jim loved it and his mother remarked that that would be his birthday cake. Most Catholic mission stations in Africa have a guest house and provide meals for travelers.

Finally they arrived at Stanleyville where they waited a day or so for SABENA (Belgian Airlines) to take them across to Leopoldville (Kinshasa) about 700 miles. The plane was a German tri-motor Junker. Believe it or not, Junker was actually the name of the company. The journey took most of the day. At Kinshasa they stayed in a guest house run by the Alliance of Protestant Missions. Jim remembers eating meals on the bank of the Congo River under the palm trees. From Leopoldville they took a train to Matadi (Congo's main port) about 300 miles. Between Leopoldville and Matadi is an impassable stretch of rapids. No person has ever navigated that stretch and lived to tell about it. At Matadi they waited a month until word came that the Portuguese ship would be coming from Angola.

During that month Kirk went back to Burundi and left Faye and the children in the hands of capable missionaries who also were trying to get to the States by the only available means. The family that watched over them was named Jenet. Jim never knew their denomination. Kirk returned to Burundi because the new work was being directed by brand new missionaries. He felt he should help them adapt to the pioneer situation. It was another year and a half before Kirk joined his family in Ohio. He showed up at Christmas time in 1945.

When word arrived that the Portuguese ship *Muzinho* was coming, the family boarded a river launch to travel to the mouth of the Congo River at a town called Boma. Next day they went on a powerful speed boat to a town called Banana. Small boats took them out to the *Muzinho* which was anchored off shore. Jim remembers being helped up the step ladder from the small boat to the deck of the large passenger ship.

Since the ship was one of few traveling from Africa and many people wanted to leave, they ended up with three times as many people as room capacity would allow. People doubled up in their rooms; some slept in the hall. It was crowded. At first, the Kirkpatrick family had a room in the back of the ship by the rudder assembly. Since the ship was old, the rudder machinery clattered with every wave, thus keeping Faye from sleeping. The children probably slept through it. After many trips to the purser, they finally got a room by the kitchen. It was a better living situation for Faye who prepared oatmeal for the children every day. Oatmeal and the special pan to cook it were in her suitcase. That pan traveled back and forth across the Atlantic with her. However, their room was right above the laundry where the machines ran constantly. The second situation was still noisy but better than back by the rudder. Jim has been fascinated with ship engines ever since. On the ship he would stand at the door of the engine room and watch the huge steam cylinders working.

They finally arrived at Lisbon, Portugal, and had to wait there for a month before they got a ship to Philadelphia. The younger children had their first taste of ice cream in Lisbon. Jim was amazed at how quietly the taxis ran on the paved streets of the city. During that month they visited castles and other historic sites. Once the whole missionary group (People who were traveling on the ship and waiting to go to to the States) took a train to Oporto, Portugal's second city. Jim remembers looking at all the sights, especially the cork and manila rope piled on the dock. Portugal exports both.

At the end of the month they started their voyage to Philadelphia on a sister ship to the *Muzinho*. It was called *Colonio*. Again the ship was crowded, this time with the missionary group, business people, and refugees from different countries affected by World War II. Next door to them was a large family from eastern Europe whose matriarch died at sea. Such wailing by the whole family Jim had never heard. Jim remembers the funeral service as they crowded up onto the deck. After prayers one of the ship's winches lifted the white coffin and lowered it gently into the ocean.

During the Atlantic crossing somebody said they saw lights following their ship under the surface of the water. Rumors were that it was a German submarine checking them out. They found out later what the submarine was up to. Jim remembers the long passage up the Delaware Bay to Philadelphia. The wharf where they docked at Philadelphia was anything but desirable. The buildings were dingy, the water was smelly, but the American officials would not let them off the ship. They sat there for two weeks under the pretext that they were quarantined because of rats on the ship and other possible contagions. Actually it turned out there were two German spies on board. Authorities were trying to figure out who they were. The submarine that had followed them had signaled someone on the ship and the ship's authorities had picked up the signal. When the authorities figured out who the spies might be by process of elimination, all the passengers were herded onto buses with none of their belongings and locked up in a hotel for the day. The authorities were able to search the ship. They found what they were looking for: spying equipment, radios, codes and many other things. The two spies were promptly arrested and the other passengers were able to disembark.

That night the Kirkpatricks stayed with friends who were their missionary supporters living in the Philadelphia area. The next day they boarded the Pennsylvania Railroad train and headed to Mansfield, Ohio. They arrived in Mansfield at noon the following day. Because of confusion about the train on which they would arrive, no one was at the station. It took more than one taxi to carry all of them and their baggage. What a welcome! They had been traveling for nearly five months.

Jim and Tim were soon treated at Mansfield General Hospital for their head infections. Several X-ray treatments finally cured them after a long four-year siege.

When they left Burundi in April, Faye was sick with symptoms indicating T.B. When she was examined in Mansfield, doctors found scar tissue in her lungs indicating she had had T.B. but the disease was gone! Faye had been healed on the way home.

The city newspaper, the Mansfield News-Journal, sent reporters to interview these amazing travelers from Africa. Jim has to admit that the photo published on the front page showed a pretty bedraggled family!

Soon after their arrival Faye decided she would take her sons for a treat at Isaly's Ice Cream Parlor in Mansfield. She ordered them banana splits. They dawdled over that special dessert and finally told their mother, "The next time could we please have our bananas with the skins on."

The family lived with Faye's parents, Grandpa and Grandma Craig, until Kirk returned from Africa. Then they moved to Kirk's mother's home in the same neighborhood. She lived alone and was blind. Her home was right next door to Kirk's sister's home. The sister regularly looked in on and helped her mother.

Byron Crouse lent Jim's folks a camping trailer. Jim's dad had bought a used, underpowered Plymouth car that was hardly able to pull the trailer. That trailer is where they slept when they went to speak in interdenominational holiness campmeetings and supporting churches in the summer.

Because they had been in Africa, teachers and parents concluded that Jim should start with kindergarten at Bowman Street Elementary School. He lasted there four days and was quickly moved to first grade. It was a godsend. Mrs. Kuppinger was a gifted teacher who could motivate almost anyone to do his best. Second grade was a down time. Jim felt as though he was in a fog most of that year. Third grade went very well. He went to fourth grade for one month but by that time the family was busy getting ready to go back to Africa with masses of boxes and supplies. The mission was coming to life after World War II and equipment and supplies were needed. During that furlough, there were many happy times getting acquainted with family and friends.

The family started their journey back to Africa at the beginning of October 1947. They traveled from New York on a Liberty troop ship that had not yet been renovated to serve as a passenger ship. To Jim's dismay, Don got to stay with his dad up in a stateroom where men and teen-age boys were lodged. Jim, Tim, and Bob had to stay down in the barracks below deck in one big room with women and younger children. Jim remembers whiling away the mornings watching women put on their makeup. Then the women would go up and sit on the deck all day with their husbands and smoke. All that those women had to go through to try to look pretty amazed Jim. Every now and then there would be a showing of a current film brought for the voyage. That's where Jim first saw "It's a Wonderful Life." More to the point, they were supposed to be home-schooling. Kirk ordered the famous Calvert Course study program, but he got fourth year for Jim and third year for Tim which were the equivalent of fifth and fourth grades, so Jim and Tim both ended up skipping one year of grade school. Jim devoured the science book but at nine years of age, he revolted against the theory of man coming from apes. Jim took his concern to his mother who said he was right.

As they entered the Mediterranean Sea they were standing on the starboard side when one of the young men pointed out The Rock of Gibralter. Jim didn't know what that meant, but he has always remembered seeing it.

They traveled to Beirut, Lebanon, then Haifa, Palestine. They could not get off the boat, because there was a cholera quarantine all over the Middle East. They finally got off the ship at Alexandria, Egypt, and took an overnight train to Cairo 140 miles.

After a few days they got booking on one of the inaugural flights of the Scandinavian Air Service to Nairobi, Kenya. They flew in a refurbished World War II bomber. Because it had radial engines, it did not fly very fast. They learned to watch their baggage. As they were boarding the bus at the hotel to go to the airport, they were swarmed by would-be porters, ostensibly to help with their luggage. Kirk and the ticket agent fended them off but they did lose one small suitcase. It contained the youngest brother Bob's change of clothes.

It took them all day to get to Khartoum, Sudan 1000 miles. When they got to the opened door of the plane to exit at 9 pm, the air from the desert felt like the blast of hot air upon opening an oven.

The next day they flew approximately 1200 miles to Nairobi, Kenya, arriving at 3 pm, where Kirk arranged for transshipment of supplies they had packed and were coming by boat. Also included were a Ford station wagon and a jeep with two trailers to be pulled by the vehicles. After business in Nairobi, they proceeded upcountry to their house near Kericho 180 miles. They stayed there one month while Kirk and Don went to Mombasa, Kenya, about 530 miles down the coast to receive the shipment and clear customs.

By early December they were ready to travel. The Ford was pulling a big army trailer with over a ton of boxes and trunks. Kirk drove the Ford. The jeep was driven by an African driver Daniel who hailed from Tenwek. Tenwek is where Kirk had planted churches and taught some of the early WGM pastors while they lived and worked in Kenya. The trailer being pulled by the jeep was of post-World War II construction, not very strong with half a ton of freight. They drove first to Kampala, Uganda, 225 miles and stayed in the old Anglican Mengo Guest House where they had stayed many times when Jim was younger. Don was born in Mengo Hospital in Uganda in 1933. On this journey the folks went to visit Marie Heinemann, a WGM missionary, who had just had surgery for a stomach ulcer. They continued on after a few days crossing the Kagera River entering Tanganyika, now known as Tanzania. The Ford arrived at the government center of Biharamuro approximately 300 miles, but the jeep and trailer had not followed.

After awhile Daniel and Don showed up in the jeep without the trailer. The trailer as mentioned was of post-war construction and weak. The tongue between the trailer and the jeep had broken. The trailer had turned over on its side in the ditch by the side of the road. Kirk, Daniel and Don took boards and rope and jerry-rigged a tongue so the trailer could be pulled to Biharamuro where they were staying.

They were lodged in a two-room government guest house. The next day Kirk and Daniel took the broken trailer hitch to a town called Bukoba to get it welded. It was Christmas Eve. On this trip, the family was among strangers. Fortunately they were able to find a welder willing to help them. When they got back, they found out the bridge was out on the road they were to travel to Burundi. So they spent Christmas in the government guest house instead of with friends in Burundi who were waiting for them. Christmas morning Faye sent the kids out to find a Christmas tree. They found a wait-a-bit thornbush. It is a small bush with many thorns. It was called "wait-a-bit" because a person has to wait a bit to pull out the many thorns. It would not stand alone so they propped it up with a stick in a bucket of dirt. Along the way Faye had bought a small kerosene stove just in case. That stove was a godsend. Faye had her one small cookpot so they had to eat in shifts. They had one bottle to bring kerosene from the local store. Jim remembers making many trips to the store.

What about presents? Jim and Tim had noticed that Kirk had put two presents for them in a certain trunk. Kirk did not remember it, but at the boys' insistence, he opened the trunk and there they were. The gifts were Mecano, the British version of the erector set that Marie Heinemann had given to the boys.

Finally the family got word that the bridge was repaired and they could travel. When they got to the bridge in question, it was a work in progress. After a couple hours, they had it fixed enough so the vehicles could cross over.

On New Year's Eve of 1947 they crossed into Burundi at sunset. They spent that night at Murehe at the new WGM mission station near the border (220 miles). Bill and Ruth Cox had expected them at Christmas but they celebrated a week later. After a few days they continued on to Kayero with Bill Cox escorting them 120 miles.

Remember that eight miles they walked to Kayero when Jim and Tim were small? The road had been built to Kayero during the folks' first term in Burundi. When the road was finished, Kirk was to meet the Belgian administrator who was to be the first to travel down the new road. (In colonial days there was a Belgian governor for all of Ruanda-Urundi. The countries were divided up into districts. Each district's head person was called an administrator.) When the administrator did not show up, Kirk did the honors.

During 1948 the family lived at Kayero. It is on a ridge in the center of the eastern side of Burundi. In April of that year, Jim gave his heart to the Lord around his tenth birthday. He dreamed Jesus had come and he was not ready. When he woke up, he breathed a sigh of relief and determined he was going to be ready. He thought of going to wake up his parents to pray for him, but he was sleeping in the camper about 100 feet from the house. In those days there was a possibility of leopards and hyenas outside, so Jim was afraid to go over to the house in the night. In any case he knew how to be saved. He had heard this many times in children's meetings and family devotions. So Jim sat up in bed and started to pray. Evidently the Lord was guiding him, for the right words came out. He prayed that he wanted to be ready, for Jesus to forgive his sins and for Jesus to come into his heart. Then he thanked the Lord for saving him and went back to sleep. Since then he has had a determination to stay close to the Lord so as to be ready when Jesus does come.

During that same year they had the first retreat at Kumbya, a peninsula on the most beautiful lake in Africa, Lake Kivu near Kibogora mission station in Rwanda. It is about 240 miles from Kayero to Kumbya. Kirk and J.W. Haley, pioneer Free Methodist missionary, discovered the premises and asked the Belgians for it for an interdenominational missionary retreat center. Kirk was ill at the time for the retreat, so the rest of the family found rides with others. Missionaries could take a vacation at Kumbya anytime, but every year there was a scheduled time for missionaries to meet together for a week of services with preaching and singing and praying together. By the time Jim and I got to Africa, African church leaders wanted missionaries to go to Kumbya for the services. They felt the missionaries were encouraged by the time together. The Alliance of Protestant Missions which owned the property, was made up of five of the missions operating in Rwanda and Burundi: the Anglicans, the Danish Baptists, the Evangelical Friends, the World Gospel Mission and the Free Methodists. Other missions participated occasionally.

During the summer of 1948, the family made a partial move to a new mission station at Murore in northeast Burundi. Jim and his brothers lived for the next year and a half in a large pyramid tent that somebody had set up. The tent did not seem very secure when they could hear the hyenas howling at night. Even if hyenas were miles away, the boys still wanted to bury their heads under the blankets. Jim says they were not in danger; it was just a Halloween-like scare.

Kirk was helping George Luce get the hospital station started. George Luce was a son of Albert Luce, the founder of the Blue Bird Bus Company, and later George became a vice president of the company. Sometimes they would be back at Kayero. Jim remembers Christmas and New Year's Eve of 1948 were spent at Kayero. George Luce was an engineer and a pilot. Even though he was with the Blue Bird Bus Company, George came out to get the hospital built for his cousin, Dr. David Stewart. He spent a number of years working on this. The hospital served a large population along the border of Burundi with Tanzania.

Don and Jim were together alone at Kayero in the old house over New Year's. On New Year's Day, Don and Jim went down to the Nyamabuye River to see if they could catch some fish. They caught nothing. A rain came up and they tried to shelter under a big mahogany tree. They were not in much of a hurry to go home, but they should have been. Suddenly they realized it was night. There is very little twilight in the tropics. Because of being at the equator, the sun is more or less directly overhead. As such there is not the refraction of the light shining through the earth's atmosphere that causes the long dawn or twilight as there is in the northern or southern hemispheres. They had just crossed the river and were climbing up the bank when the water upstream, from rain that had fallen earlier, came rushing behind them and the river rose two feet. By the time they were at the top of the bank, it was pitch black. The stars were shining but they did not give much light.

They finally found the main path to the mission but they weren't sure. Then they discovered another path going around the hill and decided to try that. Suddenly a family of francolin (partridges) fluttered up in front of them and startled them. That is the francolin's way of scaring off a "would be" enemy. Don was so surprised that he fell back and knocked Jim over. They found a third path going to the mission. As they walked up, they saw a lantern going down the path they should have been climbing. It was Philip, the faithful cook, who became worried enough to try to find the boys. A kerosene lantern doesn't give much light but it surely helped. They called to Philip and walked toward the light. That night after eating the supper Philip had prepared for them, they celebrated the New Year by beating drums and Jim playing his trumpet.

During 1948 Jim and Tim went to the new missionary children's school at Kibimba, a Friends Mission station (112 miles from Murore or 75 miles from Kayero); they would travel at about 30 miles an hour. They still had the Calvert Course at home, but Jim thinks he learned more at Kibimba than he would have if he had stayed home at Kayero. Their brother Don returned to Rift Valley Academy in Kenya for high school. Jim was at Kibimba for four three-month terms.

At Kibimba they had a one-room school with everyone studying the Calvert Course. They lived in the home of medical doctor Perry Rawson of the Evangelical Friends Mission. His wife Marjorie was the dorm mother. Tim and Jim shared a room with the now-famous Rawson brothers. Ed was the oldest and became an agricultural engineer and worked for many years with U.S. development projects overseas. Son Perry was the same age as Jim and was Jim's best friend. Today he is a well known pathologist. The youngest David was a deputy chief of mission in several U.S. embassies before he was U.S. Ambassador in Rwanda when the genocide happened in 1994.

The hydroelectric plant was just being developed so wiring was being put in all the houses on the station of

Kibimba. The hydroelectric plant was on the waterfall 70 feet high on the Kaniga River. One night Jim woke up to an electric light going on and off quickly. Clyde Thomas, the builder-engineer, often worked late at night to finish a project. Next morning Jim had one up on the rest of the boys and turned on the light.

As soon as they got back to Burundi, Kirk wanted Jim to learn to hunt. Jim was surprised when his dad handed him a box of 22-caliber shells and told him to go practice shooting where it was safe. In those days missionaries used guns for hunting meat to eat, rarely for protection. The only gun Jim had as a child was a b-b gun. Jim would use his dad's firearms. The boys learned to take all of Kirk's guns apart and clean them; handle them and shoot them. Later on at Rift Valley Academy Kirk gave Jim a Winchester saddle gun, the 32 special. Most of the senior boys had guns.

When he was home in Burundi, his dad let the boys work on the vehicles. Jim helped his mom with the medical care of the students. He felt like he was serving right along with his parents.

Jim was in seventh grade at the Kibimba School from September to December in 1949. It was decided Jim should go to Rift Valley Academy in Kenya, a thousand miles away with his brother Don. When they set out from Kayero in early January to go there for the new school year, Jim had a twinge of homesickness for about half a mile. Then he decided he was wasting his time being homesick. From then on he never was homesick again. The British school system is on the calendar year and begins in January. There are three terms of three months each with one month between. Whether or not the British still use that system, it is still in use in east Africa

Kirk had decided to travel through Tanzania to Bukoba, the port on the west side of Lake Tanganyika. From there the boys would have taken the boat to travel with Tanzania missionary kids on to RVA. When they got to the Burundi border, they found the Rugusi River had flooded and washed out all the bridges. The Rugusi River was a papyrus swamp and it took five bridges to get across the various channels. Papyrus was piled fifteen feet high on the roads because of the flood. It would be months before the way was open. Bridges were built with stone buttresses on each side of the river. The river was spanned by heavy eucalyptus beams. Planking was put on top of that. That night they were back home where they had started from. Next day they drove through Rwanda to Kampala, Uganda where the boys got on the train to go to RVA. The boys thought they had time to get a snack at a local shop, but the shopkeeper took so long that the train had started out of the station before they got their food. They ran and jumped on the train several cars back from the car they were supposed to be in. They then made their way up to their compartment. When Jim got to RVA, they asked him what grade he was in. He told them he had been studying in seventh grade but it was really only from September through December. They put him in eighth in Kenya.

Jim spent four years at RVA. He considered himself the luckiest boy alive. He had good friends and interesting activities, was able to hunt and hike in the forest; outstanding teachers and one of the most awesome views anywhere in the world. One teacher, Mildred Downing, had been named the teacher of the year in the state of Ohio. RVA is on the northeast slope of the Great Rift Valley. From the porch at the school, five extinct volcanoes compose a panoramic view. Occasionally Mt. Kilimanjaro can be seen 300 miles away.

The journey to and from school was always an interesting adventure. Sometimes it took a week. Going home they could take the train to Kisumu on the shore of Lake Victoria. Then they would take a steamer around the lake to Bukoba. From there they would take the mail truck to Ngara on the border with Burundi. From there they would hitch a ride on a coffee truck or Dad would come and get them at Ngara. Only once did Jim fly to Burundi. That was during August of 1952. Don had graduated in December of 1951 from RVA and worked with Dad in his building program at Mweya until the U.S. college year started in September. Kirk felt Jim needed to spend more time with Don before he went away to college. Flying was expensive.

The 1952 school year Jim was alone at RVA. Tim arrived in 1953. 1953 was the year RVA decided to follow the U.S. school schedule, which meant that the school year started in September. They still held to three month terms, so that those graduating in July would be able to go to the beginning of the university term in the U.S. Given a misordered Calvert Course, a short seventh grade, and compressing eleventh year into two terms, Jim ended up two years ahead of most fifteen-year-olds in school.

Political trouble was brewing in Kenya. The MauMau uprising had started and RVA was right on the edge of the area where there was political unrest. First term of 1952 he took turns with other boys doing guard duty at the senior boys' living quarters half a mile from campus. Single lady missionaries also lived in a large house in the same area. By the second term the situation was serious enough that they moved the senior boys into a refurbished attic on campus. When summer came, the folks decided that Jim and Tim should go to Mt. Carmel High School in the States. The danger was very real because, in the days after they left, the MauMaus decided to do a concerted attack on the Kijabe Mission, which contained RVA. The attack never happened. A prayer meeting was going on during the time of the planned attack and the rebels saw a row of angels on the railroad track above the mission station. This was reported by one of the rebels who later turned himself in to the authorities.

The one regret for Jim was not being able to graduate from RVA. Mt. Carmel was a happy place. If Jim had not gone there, he and I would probably have never met. The teachers were perhaps as good as at RVA. The view was pleasant but not as spectacular. The aunt and uncle who took Jim and Tim to Mt. Carmel wondered why on earth the folks would send them to a place like that. The rules were a little stricter than RVA. At RVA boys could have girlfriends but they only met in groups.

At Mt. Carmel Jim found the way of holiness. Many students at RVA were trying to live the Christian life, but they knew little about the deeper life in the Spirit. Jim felt it was an affront at RVA if no one volunteered to sing or pray. He was determined to lead and he was counted on to pray or give devotionals, but inside Jim felt he needed a whole lot more. For the first time Jim began to understand that a person could be cleansed from all sin and filled with the Holy Spirit subsequent to being saved. Jim's dad had preached and taught this message but had taught in African languages. The African languages were not the language of Jim's heart, nor did he understand the African languages that deeply. The doctrine of sanctification was even discussed in the home but Jim never understood, so it was in the first revival meeting he attended at Mt. Carmel that he went to the altar on a Saturday night. The point of commitment was to ask God for a clean heart and to be willing to do anything or go anywhere God would lead, even consecrating to stay in the States if God so willed. When he got up from that altar at 9 pm, he knew a deep peace. More importantly, the cocky pride and hot temper were gone, as well as other issues he had been struggling with. Jim was 15 years old at the time.

After graduating from Mt. Carmel in 1954, the logical thing was to go to KMBI. Jim always knew he would be a preacher from his earliest consciousness. Now colleagues began to ask where he would preach. One morning at breakfast at KMBI, those at the table said, "Surely you must be called to be a missionary. You know the mission field and you have a love for missions." In prayer that night Jim asked God, "What about this that others are saying?" The answer was a quiet sense of "Okay, you can go to Africa."

That summer while working at KMBI Jim was with Eldon Neihof on a truck trip. Eldon said, "If I were you, I would consider that little Martha Fruth." Jim nodded but did not tell him he was already thinking about it. Martha was planning to go to KMBI in the fall. Of all the girls on campus called to be missionaries to Africa, she was "number one" in Jim's opinion. But Jim said he did not want to pick the "rare orchid" without divine permission. One night in October, as he was walking from the dining hall to the Administration building, there was a clear thought, almost like a voice that told him Martha was the one. Now how was he to go about starting the relationship? To start dating her during first semester would seem like rushing it to some.

Always at the beginning of second semester, there would be a revival meeting when couples would devote time to prayer and not to dating. So Jim decided to initiate the effort after the revival meeting. Secrecy and surprise were of utmost importance to Jim for some reason. Jim was impressed with how Robert Cundiff started his relationship with Ruth Davis. (Robert sent for Ruth, saying he wanted to talk to her about the songs they were to lead in chapel, so the person sent did not know he was really asking Ruth for a date.) First of all, permission had to be granted by the dean of women who always asked questions about equal calling, similar experience and compatibility. After that Jim needed to find a way to get word to me so that we could talk. At the end of study time in the library, Jim waylaid my roommate Agnes Creed Neihof and sent her to get me. He wanted to ask me for our first date.

V.L. Kirkpatrick Family
Back row: Jim, Tim, Kirk and Don
Front row: Faye & Bob

Chapter 5

Africa-bound

At a tea party with Gerald and Marlene Bates, Kirk mentioned that he had a son and daughter-in-law who wanted to be missionaries in Africa. Gerald picked up on it and wrote a letter home to Winona Lake, Indiana, (Free Methodist headquarters), to the Free Methodist Mission Board. Soon we were contacted by Clyde Van Valin, who was then pastor of the Free Methodist Church in Wilmore, Kentucky, where we were living and studying. We made a trip to Winona Lake for an interview and within two weeks we joined the Free Methodist Church. We felt like we had come home. W. D. Cryderman was then conference superintendent in Southern Michigan. His son Bill was graduating in the same class with Jim at Asbury seminary. When the family came for Bill's graduation, they also came to visit us. When we first were contacted, I told Jim I knew nothing about the Free Methodists. Jim knew about them because his parents had worked with them from their beginning in Burundi. He assured me that they took good care of their missionaries.

Through all our years serving with Free Methodist World Missions, we found that to be true.

At Southern Michigan Annual Conference of the Free Methodist Church in 1962, we were appointed to the Pulaski Free Methodist Church, with the knowledge that it was just for a short time and then we'd be off to Africa. Jim was the first full-time pastor at Pulaski. We followed John Hyndman. a Canadian who had been working there for years. Hyndmans had their own house. A beautiful church had been built. Pulaski is near Spring Arbor Free Methodist Church and University, so for years Pulaski had been a place where students would go to help start a church in a store front. Charles Kingsley, our dear friend and supporter, was instrumental and influential in getting that church started. It was the only church in the township. The Methodist Church in town had closed years earlier. The building continued in use as a meeting place. The Pulaski Free Methodist church members rented an old house across the street from the church for us to live in. Pulaski is a small village and the the natives pronounce it *pool-ask-eye*.

The people were easy to love. Richard and Barbara Ackerman's three beautiful daughters would babysit for Beth when we needed someone. The eldest, Connie, was actually the babysitter, but they were all special to us and remained so through all the years. Edith Densmore had been the church treasurer and continued our two years there. I babysat her grandson, who was Beth's age, during weekday work hours.

When we had pastored for one year, we were called to Winona Lake, Indiana, along with another couple who were missionary candidates. We were interviewed by the mission board. Those were the days when the saints prayed on their knees until they "prayed through" on an issue. I still remember the shouts of praise as they felt they had prayed through on which couple was to go right away to the new mission work in Congo. The other couple was chosen. We had been in seminary activities together with them. Of course, I compared us to them, trying to figure out what they had that we did not have that caused them to be chosen instead of us. He had won awards as a World Book salesman. They were very conservative in how they used their money—no set of dishes, just cast—offs from the used store. No bed in their house trailer, just a mattress on the floor. We had everything our hearts desired, but it was all provided. We hadn't spent money nor begged for it. I could not figure out why we were not chosen. I felt like it was the end of our going to Africa.

We went back to Pulaski, determined to be faithful to our appointment. That second year was the high point of our lives up to then. I had an idea to work with the youth in the community in a program to help them. Some of the program we made up ourselves, such as personal hygiene training, visits from the Free Methodist physician that lived nearby, and visits from a policeman The youth even got to examine his car. The rest of the program was prepared by Free Methodist headquarters. Occasionally, we would take youth to a regional youth rally or a sporting event. The youth were responsive. There were 70 in the group. We had poor people in the community as well as rich. It was amazing how they responded to the gospel. Jim scheduled a revival meeting with Dr. Warren C. McIntire as evangelist. God's Spirit was poured out that week in a wonderful way. The Sunday school superintendent testified afterward that, before he was sanctified during that meeting, he had been like a V-8 engine operating on four cylinders and without power. In those days Sunday school attendance was high and competitive in Christian circles. Our first year there our church won the award for the greatest percentage increase in attendance and our church won Sunday-school-of-the-year award in 1964. Our second daughter Margaret Alice was born May 6, 1963, while we were at Pulaski. I still remember how Conference Superintendent W. D. Cryderman, who later became bishop, worked at pledges in campmeeting until our support, appliances and car were all pledged by Southern Michigan Conference. We felt loved and responsible to the conference to do our best for God and for them. The conference continued to support us at the same level all the time we were missionaries, i.e., 41 years. However, a couple ladies at Pulaski did say that they could let us go to Africa but no way did they feel we should take those precious little girls there.

We made headlines in the mission through no credit to us. We were the last to be appointed under Dr. Byron Lamson as General Secretary of the General Missionary Board and the first to go out under Dr. C. D. Kirkpatrick. Sometimes people who did not know our families well would in years following say they knew why the church was growing so fast in Central Africa. It was because Dr. Kirkpatrick was pouring money into that area because his son was there. Not true! We were not relatives of Dr. Kirkpatrick. However, we celebrate him and his wife, Ivanelle, even now for their concern for missions and missionaries. We arrived in Africa just after the World Fellowship of Free Methodist Churches had been formed. The World Fellowship eventually became the Free Methodist World Conference. It was/is made up of bishops and lay delegates from the general conferences of the Free Methodist Church all over the world. The world conference meets every four years. Any proposed changes in the *Book of Discipline* for our denomination have to be passed/approved by the World Conference before the book can be changed. The world conference has already been instrumental and influential in our church, and we are grateful because it has the power to maintain the doctrinal stand the mission churches were taught by past missionaries. Dr. Hugh White from Southern Michigan was a leader in creating the World Fellowship. It was a turning point when the work started on mission fields became truly a part of the world Free Methodist movement, and leaders of those churches had as much influence as leaders of the church in North America.

There was a problem. When we tried to pass the physicals to go to Africa, Margi was anemic. The physician felt we needed to stay in the States until we found out if she would respond to treatment. At the end of the conference year, we moved in with my mom and dad at the farm until we were cleared to go. Instead of leaving for Belgium for French study in the summer of 1964 as planned, we left in October.

The day we got on the train in Toledo, Ohio, the first leg of our journey to Europe, the other missionary couple who had been sent to Africa instead of us arrived back in the States. They had resigned from their appointment. I have always wondered what would have happened to us if we had been the couple chosen after one year in the pastorate. Would that year have been too difficult for us too? It was quite a coincidence that their leaving and our going happened on the same day.

It took ten days to cross the Atlantic. Jim served as chaplain on the ship. We were on the S. S. Maasdam, a Dutch luxury ship. I had always had trouble with motion sickness traveling in the hills of Kentucky, so I knew to be careful on the ocean. From the beginning I took a fourth of a Dramamine pill a day while we voyaged to Europe. I couldn't convince Jim to take it with me. When we got to the Irish Sea, we were in a horrible storm. The tables and chairs were chained down in the dining room. Instead of hundreds of people coming to the dining room to eat, we were fifteen. Jim and the girls were as sick as could be. Dramamine would not stay down long enough to be effective. It was too late to be treated. I was kept busy caring for them.

We arrived in Amsterdam in October of 1964. The mission board had pre-arranged a taxi big enough for all our baggage to take us to Brussels, Belgium. We stayed in a "pension" (boarding house) until we found an apartment to rent. Doris and Willard Ferguson, Evangelical Friends missionaries, and Harriet Wheelock Bolodar, Free Methodist missionary, were there to greet us and help us get started. We found a ground floor apartment with a small backyard where the children could play. It had no refrigerator and we requested one. The landlord bought us an apartment-sized unit. We bought groceries once a week at a supermarket, as is still our custom. The landlord felt we were spending a lot of money on food when he saw us carry the bags into the apartment. He followed the European custom of going to market every day for groceries, especially perishables. The concept is that if food is fresh, it does not need refrigeration. Refrigeration was considered a luxury; even a needless luxury. The month of December our landlord, who bought small amounts of food each day, and we, who shopped once a week, kept account of how much we had spent. We had two small children; they were only two adults. We had a turkey for Christmas and had guests in; they went out with friends. The landlord found out that our total was less than his! From then on he made his weekly trip to Bon Marche to buy his food, like we did. When we left for Africa, he moved the refrigerator to his apartment.

A Billy Graham Crusade came to Brussels while we were there. We took our Catholic landlord to the crusade. He was very interested and wanted to read the Bible, but he understood that it was against the rules in the Catholic Church for him to own a Bible. Jim went to a Catholic priest to find out what the rule was. We found out that after the Vatican Council of 1963, Bible reading was encouraged in the Catholic Church. We presented the landlord and his wife a Catholic Bible. The husband trembled as he received it. Bible reading was an exceptional concept. For years after that our landlord wrote to us regularly at Christmas to tell us the number of the page he was on in his Bible and what was happening on that page. When it came time for us to leave to go to Burundi, he and his wife came to say good-bye. His eyes were red and wet. He would not admit he was crying. When his wife asked, he said he was having trouble with his eyes that day.

Doris and Willard Ferguson were special too. We shared a double stroller. Their son Dean and our Beth were the same age and their daughter Dawnita and our Margi were the same age. It was Dawnita who gave Margaret the name Margi. From the time I read *Little Women* by Louisa May Alcott when I was twelve years old, I planned to have two girls named Beth and Meg. But when Margi was born, Meg seemed like an adult's name, so we called her Margaret until we met Dawnita who called her Margi. It stuck for all of us. She remained Margi until she moved to Washington State as an adult, where she became Meg as I had hoped.

Back to that stroller, both families used it to haul our laundry to the laundromat. I have a special memory of walking home after midnight on New Year's Eve from playing

Monopoly with the Fergusons. We were pushing that stroller with our two sleeping girls in it.

I will always be thankful we were sent to Belgium first to immerse in the culture before we went to Burundi. Immersion paved the way for me to adapt in Africa. Jim had been away from Africa for eleven years for schooling, finding a wife, and entering the pastorate. Visiting with Willard Ferguson, Jim would talk about how Burundi was when he left. Willard told him he was in for a big surprise when he got to Burundi. Willard and Doris had already been to Africa and went back to Belgium for French study. Doris was a nurse. The Fergusons first went out, I think, to be dorm parents for the missionary children. Then they went to Belgium so that Doris could take the tropical medicine course which was in French. Willard taught in secondary schools or seminary after their tour in French. The tropical medicine course was part of the Burundi government requirement for medical personnel to be qualified to work in Burundi, Rwanda and Congo. They could have taken it in other countries that provide it, but since the government papers and teaching were all in French in these countries, it was to their advantage to have French. I remember a doctor who wanted to come work without studying French. We were without a missionary doctor in Burundi, and the director of missions announced to the missionaries in a meeting in Bujumbura where all the missionaries were present that this doctor did not want to study French. I asked him why they were allowing it. His answer was, "Do you want a doctor with no French or no doctor?" He came without French but later studied it on home assignment.

Jim's parents were handicapped because they did not have French. French was the official language of central Africa. All educated people spoke French. It is really a "mixed bag." People have a tendency to mix French with their local language, so anywhere outside of that country people would have difficulty understanding them. (The same thing happens in countries where the official language is English.) We learned Belgian French, because Belgium "controlled" central Africa after World War I. Those countries continued to require the tropical medicine course for missionaries to be certified to work in central Africa. Then after they arrived in the central African country, they would have to do a practicum in a government hospital before they were allowed to work in the mission medical establishment. All the time we were there, those persons received a financial allowance from the government which was funneled back into the mission medical establishment to help buy medicine and pay national medical personnel.

Jim had two years of French in high school. I had two years of Latin. Learning another language in high school helped me learn French, but I knew no French when I went to Belgium. We studied in different classes at different times for two reasons. One, I had to start at absolutely the beginning. Jim was already acquainted with French and had heard it spoken in Burundi. The other reason was we took turns staying with the children. Jim went to school in the mornings and came home in the afternoons. I went to school in late afternoon and came home in the night. We had wonderful private tutors. I learned the most from them. Private tutor and class would be all in the same trip on the tram (trolley). In Burundi, I took classes at the Alliance Francaise in Bujumbura until we went on home assignment. When I was in bed for a month with Hepatitis E in Seattle, I studied French on tapes while I lay in bed.

An interesting note about Brussels is that all along the streets there were small shops that sold varieties of only one thing, such as chocolate or jewelry or hats. I remember complaining to Jim that it seemed like the clerks were guarding their wares and really did not want to part with them at any price. Also included in the shops were bakeries. We liked the bread still warm, but the clerks at the bakery told us that warm bread was not good for a person and it would make us sick. We argued about this more than once and usually received the bread warm (won the debate). Most Belgians liked coffee; our tutor would almost always serve us coffee with our lesson. Belgium was famous for the making of lace. I bought some for gifts, I recall. That too was sold in those small shops.

In Brussels there was an office of Protestant Missions where they helped us to get visas to go to Africa. I don't remember how we got paid. I think our salary was put in our U.S. bank account by the mission. I do remember that in those years we were only paid every three months. The mission paid our living expenses, including our food while we were in language study. That was quite a surprise to us but we kept track diligently of everything we bought.

Walking in Brussels was an interesting experience. One could always tell who lived in each house. The sidewalk in front of a Flemish house was scrubbed every morning, but not so with the French. And we were told more than once that the dog population in Brussels was greater than the people population.

My biggest complaint about Belgium was they were too bureaucratic. Every place you went from the bank to the post office to the laundry demanded paper work and not just one paper. When we got to Burundi and applied for visas or drivers' licenses or to rent, which all required pages to fill out, people who did not know Belgium would say, "This is

Africa." My answer always was, "This is not Africa. This is the influence of Belgium during colonial days."

We were asked to leave Belgium earlier than originally planned because Dr. Len and Marti Ensign were coming home to the States, leaving Doris Moore alone at the Kibuye Hospital and station. We were to go and study the Kirundi language at Kibuye. Kirundi is the African language of Burundi. Betty Ellen Cox was to be our language teacher. She lived at Kibimba, the Friends mission station where there was a hospital and the teacher training school. She was teaching there at the time. We made a trip once a week for a language lesson with Betty Ellen. Jim already knew some Kirundi, so we had two lessons: one for Jim and one for me. I sat and listened to his. Jim usually went out and found an African to talk to while I had my lesson. Beth and Margi sat and played quietly with Betty Ellen's stuffed frog named Apamenandus and a little stuffed dog named Pug. Betty Ellen and I sat at her nearby table for my lessons. The rest of the days of the week I had pronunciation lessons with Mariya, a nurse at the hospital. I would read or say words and read Scripture over and over and Mariya would correct me. It took a special relationship for an African to correct a white woman, but I had that with Mariya. African women are more withdrawn than white women in public, but they can really let their husbands or children "have it" when they think no one can hear. An African woman would never speak up to correct anyone in those days. Sometimes we would meet with Doris for lessons but not often. If I had a question that could not wait till we saw Betty Ellen, I would ask Doris Moore, the nurse. Doris was busy running the hospital. Every day I would write out the answers to a lesson. Then Betty Ellen would correct all I had done when I visited her the following week. Besides language study for one year, we were required to memorize a list of Scriptures in Kirundi, translate a number of hymns and the Gospel of Mark into English from Kirundi, and take an oral and written exam before we could become voting members of the mission. I made it in spite of two moves and instability in the country. For a year the U.S. Embassy instructed us to keep suitcases packed so that we could evacuate at a moment's notice. They were to notify us via *Voice of America Radio.* From that time on I decided to live it up and use good sheets and good towels and not save them for company. Who wants to skimp and leave the best for intruders?

When we first got to Africa, we both were surprised at how much nicer missionary homes were than African church leaders' homes were. One time I said, "I wish I lived in a house like yours. I don't like it that ours is nicer than yours." The church leader said, "Oh, no. We are happy that you have a good house. We just want our house to be like yours." Of course, by the time we arrived we did have electricity from 6 to 9 p.m. from a diesel generator and water pumped to our house. To heat water for baths, we had a barrel set in bricks and cement where a fire was built every night to heat the water.

A dock strike took place in New York when we left the States. Our shipment did not leave the States until we arrived in Burundi after five months of French study in Belgium. We were very thankful we could use Ensign family's things and live in their house till ours arrived. As providence would have it, our shipment did come when it was time for Dr. Floyd and Alice Hicks to arrive from Canada for him to be the doctor at Kibuye. They moved into the doctor's housewhile we moved into Doris Moore's house, and she moved into the first house built up closer to the hospital.

The political climate was very unstable in the country. Hutu leaders were taken and killed, never heard from again. I was so afraid of the situation that it made me sick. The nurse gave me shots of some kind for headaches and stomach aches, but they did not make any difference. One night at 1 a.m., I was standing at the window in our bedroom watching the military trucks lumber by on the road down below. It was all the more noticeable because there was a curfew and nobody was to be outside of their homes after 6 pm. I was positive they were going to come to our mission station and take the nurses and other hospital workers. As I stood there crying, Jim and our two daughters were fast asleep. Suddenly I remembered parts of Psalm 34:4 and 6: "This poor man called, and the Lord heard him and he delivered me from all my fears." Just like that, my headache disappeared, my stomach didn't hurt anymore, and I was relaxed. I lay down in the bed beside my husband, fell fast asleep, and slept till morning. I was truly delivered from all my fears. Much worse things were ahead of us, but I never again had the same fear I had before God touched me.

Kirk had packed belongings up in the attic of the missionary children's school dorm at Mweya for our arrival. Pat and Tim already had some of Kirk's belongings in their apartment in Bujumbura. They got there before us to work in the Christian radio station in the capital. Kirk was quite concerned that we had spent money on a new mattress to take to Africa. He felt we didn't need a new one, because the one he took out in 1934 was "the Cadillac of mattresses." Kirk thought his mattress was still good enough for us. Now it was March of 1965. Also he said that if he had sold those things to other missionaries, he would have received $1000 for them. As it was, he gave it all to his sons. Kirk and Faye were living at the time in the Airstream trailer at Mweya and didn't need big furniture. George and June Janes at Pulaski had given us a wood stove in wonderful condition, which we used all the time in high altitude homes. We bought two easy chairs and a sofa while at Pulaski and used them in Africa until 1994. I suppose someone is still using them at Kibogora. I don't think they were stolen in the war.

We lived in our second home at Kibuye for one month. I fully expected to live out our days in Africa in that house. However, a surprise was in store for me. Jim Johnson, a Free Methodist missionary, was put under house arrest at Muyebe. Muyebe was the oldest, as well as the largest, Free Methodist Church in Burundi. That is where J. W. Haley, founder of the work in Burundi, lived. There was only one foundation stone remaining from the four years the Germans had a mission station there before World War I. J.W. Haley built the first two houses. His son-in-law Burt McCready built the shop and the third house. Ron Collett started building the large church and could not finish it because of illness.

We depended on short wave radios like we depend on telephones here in the States. We were to take a language exam on the same day we were notified to turn in our radios to the local government office. That meant Jim had to turn in the radio for Muyebe. He took parts out of the set so that the radio was useless when the officials did get it. It ended up I made a higher grade in the language exam, but everybody knew that Jim could speak more fluently at that time than I could.

The situation when Jim Johnson was put under house arrest was quite alarming. One soldier stood outside the big living room window with a gun to Jim's head while Shirley worked with other military people in the house to search everywhere. They dumped out dresser drawers, lifted mattresses off beds, went through all the cupboards looking for guns that gossip had told the government officials Jim Johnson had stashed. They found nothing. What had caused them to accuse Jim Johnson was that he had gone to plead with the authorities to release people who had been arrested at Muyebe. Jim Johnson took off with his family for the capital Bujumbura as soon as the military was off the station. They got a flight to the States. We were asked to pack their belongings to go to the States. Gerald and Marlene Bates helped us. Then we were asked to auction off the rest of Johnsons' belongings. The Johnsons never returned to Africa. The first Sunday morning after the auction of Johnsons' things, the church was filled with people. A man came dressed in Shirley Johnson's striped red and white pajamas and paraded from the back to the front of that long church. It was all I could do not to laugh. We moved to Muyebe after spending one month in our new home at Kibuye.

After six months at Muyebe the former missionaries Stan and Eileen Lehman, who had been on home assignment, were due to come back. Stan was asked to be the maintenance man at Muyebe. Jim Kirkpatrick was elected district superintendent at Rwintare. Stan and Eileen were asked to live at Rwintare while we were living at Muyebe. It meant a lot of traveling for both families, so we agreed for Lehmans to come back to their home at Muyebe that we had been in for six months, and we moved to Rwintare. We lived at Rwintare for one year. Our son Virgil Edwin was born in April 20, 1967, during our time at Rwintare.

While we were at Kibuye Hospital for Ed's birth, the wife of primary school director at Rwintare, Mathias Kaluba, gave birth to their first child Cadet. As providence would have it,

Ed was in Africa with us when Cadet was married and got to participate in Cadet's wedding.

The mission asked us to move again to the capital to live where Gerald and Marlene Bates had been living, because the Bates were asked to move to the new work in Congo and live in Bukavu. We were asked to move when Edwin was two weeks old, but I asked for permission to wait until he was six weeks old. Permission was granted. We lived in Bujumbura for one year, arriving in the States in May 1968 so our son Leonard Wayne could be born here in Jackson, Michigan, in July. The night before we were to catch our flight, we received a telegram from Dr. C. D. Kirkpatrick asking us not to leave Africa at that time because another couple said they would leave if we did. They felt they could not live in that suburb alone. Dr. Leonard Ensign sent a telegram back that we were to get home to the States as planned because, if we waited, we could not fly until after the baby was born. As it turned out, Len was born *placenta previa* which meant that I spent a week in the hospital. I am not sure that was absolutely necessary. Our son Len was the last delivery that our Christian, former missionary doctor ever made. That birth was a stressful time for all of us. It was a good thing we were in the States for the birth.

Those were dark days for Gerald and Marlene Bates. War came to Bukavu, Congo, and their possessions were destroyed before they even had opportunity to unpack. I am sure they often wished they had stayed put in Bujumbura, Burundi, and we surely grieved to leave Rwintare. Merlin Adamson had built a beautiful home at Rwintare for missionaries to live in, thinking that would cause the church and mission to keep missionaries living there. It was at high altitude, remember, so he had built efficient fire places in the living room, the dining room and the master bedroom. The

African church was sad when we left, and we were sad. Later the church rented out that house to Europeans working with the peat moss and the experimental farm. Those workers stored the peat in the kitchen by the stove. One day the workers left for a trip to Bujumbura with something cooking on the stove. The peat got hot, caught fire and the gas bottle on the stove exploded, setting the whole house on fire. The house was demolished. The noise of the explosion was heard at the government office four miles away.

All of those moves around the country to different mission stations helped us get acquainted with African church leaders everywhere in Burundi in a more personal way than we ever would have if we had stayed on one station. We also became acquainted with the Free Methodist Churches all over the country. Our first term was a real preparation for the following terms.

Maybe you are wondering if I am giving you the real reasons we moved so often. Well, I am! Jim and I felt strongly that the will of the board, African and missionary, was the will of the Lord. Besides, if we refused to cooperate with the will of the group, what kind of example would we be presenting to a church which we were trying to teach the importance of servant-leadership?

When we arrived back in the States, we lived in a mobile home on my mom and dad's farm for one year. It was a great time of bonding for our children with their grandparents and aunts and uncle who were still at home. While Jim traveled in deputation, visiting churches, I stayed at home with the children. Beth brought chicken pox home from school; two weeks later, Margi had it and then Edwin and Len. After six weeks of my staying in the trailer, caring for sick children, Dad came over to our home and said he was staying home with the children that Sunday while I went to church.

In those days the mission board arranged our schedule to return to the field. July 4, 1969, arrived all too quickly. We were to fly from Mansfield, Ohio's small airport to Cleveland. The Mansfield Free Methodist Church loaded us down with hand luggage: stuffed toys for the children, brownies for a snack, and more. From Cleveland we traveled to New York where we found all flights on hold because of a strike by fuel truck drivers. We had to wait until enough fuel could be found to cross the Atlantic Ocean. It was hot. The lounges were packed with waiting people. It was impossible to get to the counter to buy food or drink because of the crowd. Everyone passed orders and money to the counter through others and then the food was passed back. I was amazed at people's honesty and patience. Jim wiggled through the crowd with our Beth and Margi and took them for a walk outside while the boys and I sat on our luggage to guard it. Dr. Herbert Sebree was pastor of the Spring Arbor Church in Michigan. His daughter traveled with us to do a stint with the VISA program of the Free Methodist Church. It was a volunteer short-term mission program that still exists. She was amazed at the patience of our children, but wondered why on earth we would take little children to Africa. Finally our SABENA flight was announced with the assurance that we would find enough fuel in Newfoundland for us to cross the ocean, so we stopped in Newfoundland for refueling on our way to Brussels, Belgium. After a layover in Brussels of some hours, we continued our journey to Bujumbura, Burundi.

THE VIRGIL E. KIRKPATRICK
FAMILY

Our children, Beth, Margi, Ed and Len

Chapter 6

African Culture

Two missionaries had the reputation for knowing the Kirundi language and culture the best when we got to Burundi. They were Free Methodist Betty Ellen Cox, a U.S. citizen, and Church Missionary Society (Anglican) Rosemary Guillebaud, who was British. Rosemary had translated the Bible from English into Kirundi, and Betty Ellen proof-read it. They worked with Africans to be sure of the correct translations. The presentation and inauguration of the translation was introduced after we moved to Bujumbura during our first term. It was a great day of celebration for the Protestant churches in Burundi.

Rosemary also wrote a book *The African Doctrine of God Ruanda-Urundi in* about 1945 (when I was seven years old). During colonial days before independence was declared, Ruanda-Urundi was considered under one government and those were the names of the two countries. After independence was declared, the names were changed to Rwanda and Burundi. I very much appreciate Rosemary's book, because it lends credence to what I have heard from Africans myself.

Rosemary quotes Dr. Stanley Smith in writing about the religious system of the people in Rwanda and Burundi. Dr. Smith was an Anglican medical doctor, pioneer missionary, revivalist, and contemporary of Jim's father. Jim knew him when he was a child. Smith said, "They (the people of Burundi and Rwanda) believe in the existence of one Creator God, but their faith is more concerned with the spirits that people the underworld about them. The real motive behind all their religious ideas is solely to achieve and to maintain material prosperity. The four freedoms the primitive African covets are freedom from disease, from hunger, from poverty, and from childless marriage. These desirable blessings however, are threatened by the occult and terrifying power of the spirits. Every ill to which humanity is heir is laid at their door and the social security of the community depends on the priestly wisdom to appease its unaccountable hostility. The science of these practitioners is a compound of shrewd common sense, acute powers of observation of nature, a profound understanding of the workings of the Africa mind, and audacious roguery. They hold the souls of the people in a bondage of fear and almost unbelievable credulity."

The first missionaries had to decide what word was going to be used for God in the languages of these two countries. The Catholics decided to use the Swahili word *Mungu*, but that was a foreign word to people in the two countries. The Protestants wanted a word that the people could understand. It was finally decided to use the word *Imana,* which is also their word for "luck." Africans will say, "Ndagiz' Imana," for "I am lucky." It was also their word for the great Creator, the first cause of all good. Before the influence of Christianity, they did not fear *Imana* because He did not enter into their daily lives at all and yet He was always in their thoughts. He was not feared, because they felt He had no power to harm. In the days before Christianity, there was no cult to worship *Imana* as there was for *Ryangombe* (Rwanda) or *Kiranga* (Burundi). *Ryangombe* is a territorial spirit that originated in Rwanda. It would seem from tales about him that he was once a historical person. *Ryangombe* or *Kiranga* was/is considered malevolent and there was/is a highly organized cult in connection with his worship. They believe that this one can prevent *Imana* from helping people. So it is *Ryangombe* that must be "paid off" in order to allow a channel for God's blessing. He gives good things to those who pray to him, and preserves them from evil. *Ryangombe* or *Kiranga* is greatly feared and he is considered a sort of minister of *Imana*, carrying out *Imana*'s commissions. It is rare for the nationals to use *Imana*'s name in cursing. When it is done, it causes more grief than any other kind of curse, because He is thought of as the Parent, Friend and Creator, and not as a natural enemy.

Mizimu are the spirits of the departed. These have no power except over their own families, and when exercised, the power is always for evil. In Burundi only the grandfather or occasionally the father has any power to hurt his descendants. The *muzimu* is powerless until dissolution has taken place, thus a family has no fear of a dead relative for several months. The position and/or possessions are given to someone else. If trouble befalls the family after this period has elapsed, the head of the house goes to the witchdoctor (*umupfumu*) and asks advice. The witchdoctor usually says it is the deceased grandfather who is angry. If the person is a Hutu, he goes home and builds a little sleeping house beside the grave, and prepares food and beer. Then he calls the whole family, however widely scattered. They kneel around the hut and the grandson enters and prays and asks the grandfather to cease his anger and receive the gifts and bless them. Then they offer gifts of food ceremonially. It is different with the Tutsi. The spirits are not actually worshipped, though they are reverenced. They build the hut but not near the grave. People are not afraid of it and will shelter in it from the rain or pass the night in it.

In Rwanda the spirit of any member of the family has power to do harm. They particularly fear the spirit of a boy or girl of marriageable age, of someone who died away from home, or of an old servant who had been in the family for many years. Divination (unknown in Burundi) is practiced to discover which spirit it is without going to a witchdoctor. Bones, smoke, or chicken liver are used. Rules of divination are unclear, but if the answer did not please the family or person, they will say, "Bring another chicken or a goat, and I will divine some more." Then they build a house for the spirit to live in.

In Burundi there are three varieties of nature spirits. These are human in form and dwell in lonely places, such as outcrops of rock, steep valleys and open expanses of water. In Rwanda these spirits are not known. Rwandans have a different variety that inhabits forests, streams, and cliffs. Every person has his own personal spirit whose influence may be negligible or actively malign.

In Burundi there is a spirit called *Rwuba*, who is known as the Adversary of *Imana* or God. His origin is obscure. He has no known form. He watches his chance to do harm and his one aim is to spoil what God has made. This thought is more prominent in Rwanda. *Rwuba* is unknown there, but they have another who creates all dangerous and ugly things, and another who creates evil and useless things.

These two are considered the prime cause of evil and are said to give only to snatch away again.

There are certain agencies between man and the occult. These are witchdoctors *(bapfumu)* who have power over drugs and can do things that no ordinary mortal can do without swift retribution. The witchdoctors give drugs to kill people and are not be punished for doing so. The witch doctor is considered the worst/strongest of the people with special powers. The rainmaker or the medicine man is not considered as strong as the witchdoctor. Witchdoctors communicate with the unseen, but act apart from God (*Imana*), though they are in very close league with *Ryangombe* and carry out his wishes.

When there is lack of rain, people will go to the rainmaker to call the rain. When he acts as medicine man, he is an herbalist. Sometimes he gives herbs that really help, but sometimes he gives too strong of a dosage. Between the rainmaker and the medicine man and the witchdoctor is the diviner who can decide who did what and is able to foretell the future.

Burundi and Rwanda and Kenya nationals are still very sensitive to omens. Many birds are thought to bring bad luck if they sit on a house. Among the most feared is the owl, according to Rosemary. In Rwanda if an ibis sits on a house the family will not continue to live there.

A house surrounded or entered by pincher ants is a bad omen in Kenya. When Jim was in the States for semi-annual mission board meetings in October of 1997, the executive committee of the Kenya Free Methodist Church's women's group was to meet in our house, a duplex. The day before it was to meet our half of the house was surrounded by pincher ants. I used a whole can of insecticide trying to kill them. Both Mary, our house help, and I worked hard to keep them out of the house. The next morning our part of the duplex was again surrounded. I used another can of insecticide. Mary acted so afraid. I asked her why and she said that when this happens, it is a sign that something bad is going to happen to you. When the ladies came for the meeting, I told them our problem. They were all educated women and they all acted very uncomfortable when I told them. Finally Rachel, the chairlady, said, "Well, maybe it's because your mother is in very poor health," which indeed she was. The next day I was alone in my office at school when I received a phone call from my husband in the U.S. that Joel Kirkpatrick, our dear grandson, had been stabbed to death.

In both Burundi and Rwanda the wagtail bird is considered sacred, and his presence is a sign of blessing. It is called a wagtail because its tail flops up and down as it hops around. It is a small black and white bird with spindly legs. We had them hopping continually on our big veranda of the mission house in Kigali, Rwanda. Rosemary said that unless he visits the proposed site of a house when it is being leveled, the site is abandoned.

There are a number of taboos. Some taboos are for one country and some for the other. Example: it is taboo for a woman to whistle in Burundi or Rwanda. If she does, her husband will die. In Burundi, it is acceptable to call a child *sha,* like you would say "kid" in the U.S. In Rwanda a young fellow may use that word to refer to another young fellow, otherwise, the word means bastard.

Rosemary explains that in the breaking of a taboo, the evil consequences which follow are thought to be inherent in the nature of the taboo, and not a punishment from *Imana.*

Both languages have a word for good manners: *ikinyabupfura i*n Rwanda and *urupfasoni* in Burundi. A well-mannered woman in Burundi is called an *umupfasoni*. Some examples of good manners are as follows:

- receiving a gift with both hands, giving a gift or offering with both hands or at least using the right hand, never with the left. The left hand is considered inferior to the right hand so it would be disgraceful to receive a gift with the left hand. In days past a child could be killed if he was found to be left-handed. Left-handed people learn to write with their right hand in school, even in our time.
- code-switching. A person may have a plan to do you in, but to your face, he will act as if all is well, you are his best friend.
- to show his superiority a person might speak only in English or French, instead of the local language when he is wanting to show that he is superior to the person he is addressing.

It is always important to save face and protect your reputation in Africa. In America we say, "Sticks and stones may break my bones, but words can never hurt me." But in Burundi and Rwanda, they would rather be beaten than to have a bad word spoken about them, or to be relieved of an important position or released from work at any level. It is your identity, your place in society. With this in mind, any punishment would not be a matter of following a code; rather, it would be showing a person that what he had done was shameful.

Nursing a baby in public and wearing low-necked dresses are considered acceptable in Rwanda and Burundi, but a good woman is always covered from her waist to her ankles. When we first went to Burundi poor women worked in their gardens with only a wrap-around cloth around their waists and considered themselves covered.

Both countries have words of congratulations when a child is born. During the first few days after the birth, you say "Irakurokoye," which means "God has saved you from destruction." You could also say, "Uzabyara benshi. Uzaduha kamwe," which means "You will have many children. You will give us a little one."

There are many words for farewell also. In Kirundi you would say, "N'akagaruka," which means, "I'll see you again soon," but if you are going on a long trip or are at a funeral, you would say, "N'agasaga," which means a long or final good-bye.

The wedding ceremony was unique in both countries. There was always a go-between who would take messages back and forth regarding the bride price. An educated girl would "cost" a lot more than an uneducated one. In Burundi, when a girl married, she left everything behind in her father's home, even her clothes. The groom had to provide new clothes for her. Her father and brothers could not go to her wedding, nor could they ever enter her house, once she was married. In Rwanda it was quite the opposite. It was the joining of two families, the bride's and the groom's. The big clay beer pot would be in the center of the wedding reception with many long sturdy straws made of reeds to suck the beer. Christians continued the ceremony, but with either fresh banana juice or Kool-Aid if they were fortunate enough to be close friends with a missionary who had plenty. In recent years, cases of soft drinks would be presented for the guests along with the feast. The bride and groom would be the first to try the drink from the clay pot. Then they would drink together with other guests around the pot. We went to many weddings and almost always we were invited to drink with the bride and groom before others had used the straws. If the couple were not Christians, the reception would end with people drunk. We would not drink from the clay pot if some Christian present told us not to, meaning it was fermented.

We felt it unfortunate that beer drinking was included in every ceremony: the coming-out day for a mother and a new baby (about fourteen days after the baby was born; before that, the mother and baby stay secluded.); an engagement party; a funeral; any transaction at a government office such as the exchange or sale of land; New Year's Day, etc. The Rwanda Free Methodist Church took a strong stand against beer-drinking before we moved there. Quite a few people left the church when they did. Many returned who had gone to the Pentecostal Church and brought new members with them.

Beer is made out of a certain kind of banana that rots before it is ripe. A hollowed-out log is used to put the bananas in. Then people tramp the bananas with their feet to make the juice. When people learned the importance of killing germs, they cooked the juice which caused it not to ferment as quickly. Beer is also made from millet grain. I never learned or saw how they did that like I did the banana beer. Honey is added when it is on hand. Millet is the grain of the poor, the wealthy would starve before the poor in famine times. They made a porridge out of millet which we too would have often. Our whole family liked it. It looked like chocolate pudding but did not taste like it. Millet is a nutritious grain which we in the States would do well to use.

Africa is quickly changing because of movies and the Internet, or because families move to the city and leave their tribal neighborhood. The change is so great that languages are dying. Most families will have a corpse taken back to the tribal area when a person dies. Children will use the trade language such as Kiswahili in east Africa, Lingala in western Congo, as well as French in countries that were controlled by Belgium in colonial days, English in countries controlled by Britain in colonial days, and not even know or speak the language of their grandparents. Also the customs are quickly disappearing as the youth are more exposed to the customs of other countries.

Very important to all Africans is the concept of belonging. You only have rights to say anything about a group if you are in it. Therefore, if you leave a group, you no longer have the right to speak. As part of a group, you try to develop as many relationships as possible with important or ordinary people. To know somebody is to have power.

Any community or group has a council or group of elders who arbitrate or decide on proper maintenance of order. If you are part of the group and act apart from this leadership, you have broken code. Three examples of leadership procedures are as follows:

1. When you go into anyone's domain or territory, you go first to the leaders to let them know you are there and establish your reason for being there, even if it is just to greet them.
2. For us as missionaries to act on our own and not involve the group could cause problems. On one occasion, some missionaries were disciplined by the mission and sent home, but the Africans considered those missionaries as part of their group. Jim was asked, "Why didn't you let us counsel and discipline them instead of just sending them home? Perhaps we could have saved them and they would still be with us."

3. A certain missionary could not get along with one of his African national workers. The missionary wanted to release him, but somehow the African leaders found out about it and asked if they could give advice in the situation. The missionary's worker had been disrespectful and, from our point of view, he would have been let go. The elders' counsel was, "You the missionary are held in high regard, therefore you are the important person in this situation. In our custom it is the important person's place to show grace and mercy. By doing so, the offender will no longer offend and the important person will have established a new relationship with the offender and the community." The missionary did not understand this at all but swallowed his pride and accepted the decision of the group.

It must be noted that cultures vary from nation to nation, from tribe to tribe. The social structure of the people of Rwanda and Burundi are similar. These countries have a vertical hierarchy in their social structure, i.e., one would start with the villager who relates to the village headman, who relates to the township supervisor, who relates to the regional supervisor, and so on. In the old days the order was villager, councillor, subchief and chief. As such, one village does not relate to another village directly; they relate to the structure above them. Thus, authority is held in high regard even if you don't like the authority. It is the "yes, Boss" attitude. If the authority does reasonably well, there is no problem, and life goes on. If the authority becomes tyrannical or brutal, the system begins to fall apart.

I must add that Rwanda and Burundi have the highest population density in all of Africa. Pre-1994, there were 650 people per square mile in Burundi and 850 per square mile in Rwanda. Most of the people were agriculturalists, at least in part. In a good year life could go on. In times of famine, many suffered. Two reasons for the heavy population are as follows:

1. Because Rwanda and Burundi were organized kingdoms with standing armies, the Arab slave-holders were not able to decimate the population as they did in Tanzania, Congo, and Malawi and elsewhere. The Arab slave-holders were basically predators and only went where there was disorder or a weak social structure.

2. Rwanda and Burundi are near the equator; thus, there are at least two rainy seasons, so the people could harvest twice a year. If they had valley gardens during dry season, they could harvest three times a year.

According to anthropologists and archaeologists that have placed relics in the museum in Brussels, Belgium, and the one that was in Butare, Rwanda, when we lived there, the original people in the countries were pygmies who were hunters and gatherers. According to many experts, the first migration into the countries of Rwanda and Burundi were the Bantu peoples from West Africa, about a thousand years ago. We call these the Congo-Niger people. They spread over Africa from west to east and south across the Congo basin, as far as Angola, and along the east African highlands to south Africa. Those who migrated to Rwanda became known as the Rwandans, and to Burundi, the Burundians. These people were farmers who displaced and subjugated the pygmies.

Some 400 years ago, Nilotic herdsmen from eastern Sudan and western Ethiopia came into Rwanda and Burundi seeking pasture land for their cattle. Nilotics came from the upper Nile region, which is eastern Sudan or western Ethiopia. Some people say these are the smooth-skinned people mentioned in Isaiah 18:2, 7. Others say that reference is to people from Somalia. The Nilotics moved south from the Nile region, into Kenya, but Kenyan tribes rejected them, so they eventually arrived in Rwanda and Burundi. Eventually they adopted the local languages and lost their own Nilotic languages. Always the Congo-Niger people (Hutu) have been more populous than the Nilotic people (Tutsi). After a time the farmers noticed that the Nilotic herdsmen had an advantage because their herds produced milk, meat, skins and fertilizer. They began to attach themselves to the herdsmen by various arrangements. Eventually they became subservient to the Nilotic minority. The Nilotic peoples established kingdoms: in Burundi, a strong centralized kingdom. In Rwanda, a relatively small kingdom established relationships through alliances, conquests and marriages. Eventually they covered the territory known as modern Rwanda.

The Nilotic people will dispute the premise that they came after the Bantu. This is an effort to establish their legitimacy as rulers. They maintain that they came at the same time and are not different from the majority group posturing for political advantage. Deep differences are under the surface. In actuality the countries were made up of about 85% of the Bantu (Congo-Niger or Hutu), 14% Nilotic (Tutsi), and 1% pygmy. The name Hutu which means "servant or slave" came to be the name for the Bantu from their serfdom relationship in acquiring cattle from the Tutsis. The origin of the name Tutsi is disputed.

In Burundi in 1972 a person's tribe was decided by the origin of his father. For example, our church legal representative was the grandson of Tutsis, son of a Hutu father and Tutsi mother. His paternal grandfather married a Tutsi woman. He married a Tutsi. Because his father was a Hutu, even though he was more Tutsi than Hutu, he was killed.

Before the rampage of 1994, people tried to act as if belonging to one tribe or another did not matter. Burundi did not even distinguish on I.D. Cards whether a person was Hutu or Tutsi. In Rwanda, it had to be on the I.D. Card. We witnessed several marriages between the tribes. Young people told us they were hardly aware of the tribalism. People of the two countries tried to figure out how the two tribes could live in peace. Someone suggested that the Hutus live in one country and Tutsis in the other. One answer given was, "If we did that, who would rule the Hutus?" The Tutsis declared they were born to lead and that Hutus were incapable of leading. However, the Hutus had always placed a high priority on education. I never heard one child in Africa say they did not like school.

The Tutsis tend to be tall with high cheek bones. The Hutus tend to be shorter. I have seen a lot of tall Hutus and short Tutsis though. Sometimes it was difficult for us foreigners to know who belongs to which group but they seemed always to know.

Rosemary Guillebaud and Betty Ellen Cox

Chapter 7

M I L I E U

Many people do not know that Germans were in Ruanda-Urundi from 1905 to 1917. They were autocratic and sometimes cruel. By autocratic, I mean that the leader in a given area did not work with a governing body of any kind to make a decision. For example, if an African came to him for help, he would point his gun at the head of another African with a herd of cows or goats and tell him to give his herd to the person asking for help. Each person ruled alone with an iron hand. German missionaries were there from 1911 to 1917. That was not enough time to get much started by way of churches or mission stations.

During World War I, the Germans were defeated by a combined force of British and Belgian soldiers from East Africa and Congo. The Belgians were given Ruanda-Urundi as a League of Nations trust, and the British were given Tanzania. The Belgians already controlled the Congo. The Belgians were strict and bureaucratic. By bureaucratic I mean that leaders always worked strictly with a governing body. Thus the shelves in the government offices were stacked with yellowed tattered files left over from colonial days. It was important for us all to keep a copy of every transaction, in case someone responsible lost something and needed an invoice to prove a payment. Africans who learned from the Belgians and the pioneer missionaries were skilled in taking inventories every day to make sure every piece of paper, book, slate, and slate pencil was accounted for in the schools. Sometimes I have wondered if that attention to detail is what caused people to learn to be devious in order to obtain something. It could take a long time to run the gauntlet of all that was required to sell or buy a property and get the deed through a local government office. When independence came, with no other example of how to run things, Rwanda and Burundi continued to use the bureaucracy method. Bureaucracy fit more with the traditional Ruanda-Urundi way of governing through hierarchy. The Belgians had ruled with the respective kingdom structures, i.e., kings, chiefs, counselors, etc. They built roads and there was limited education in the Catholic parishes. They saw to it that there was improvement in agriculture, especially when they started cotton and coffee plantations, so that the cash crops could provide money for the people to pay taxes to run the government. There were limited usable natural resources in Ruanda-Urundi. Congo contains some of the world's richest reserves of natural resources. Some Belgians set up businesses. Later a number of Greeks and Arabs moved into the business sector.

Control of the population was maintained by prison terms and extensive use of corporal punishment. The whips made of hippopotamus hide were talked about many years after independence.

It was difficult to start church work in the early days because Belgium is strongly Catholic. The Roman Catholic Church was trying to establish a near monopoly in Ruanda-Urundi. Finally, the government allowed Protestant groups to occupy the sites where the German missionaries had started work. Then the monopoly was further weakened as more groups came in. There was often tension between the Catholic and Protestant groups, but after the second Vatican Council 1965, relationships between the two groups improved greatly.

In 1948, the Socialists in Belgium won a majority in parliament over the religion-based parties. Changes came soon. Whipping was banished. Educational support was broadened to include schools in the Protestant groups.

After independence the new governments tried to maintain the roads and social infrastructure. By this time the villagers saw the benefits of having a cash crop, and no longer had to be forced to grow coffee and cotton. A marked difference became evident in relationships between the Africans and foreigners. The Africans were in charge; foreigners had to "toe the line" on various government regulations. Some regulations were carry-overs from colonial days; others were new rules. In general the two groups co-existed if we foreigners remembered that we were now guests coming to work with the people. As much as possible, we tried to work through our African colleagues, letting them represent us in getting necessary legal work or documentation. Jim and I spent our time in Africa reminding each other that we were visitors and we were to act like it. We loved Africa and the Africans, but a visitor does not control. We only helped with the work when we could.

Underlying this picture was the tribal problem. Colonialism had brought a forced peace to the various countries. Independence was seen as not just freedom from colonial powers, but fewer restrictions on one's reaction to people of another ethnic origin. In Africa one often hears the proverb, "Blood is thicker than water." Whatever one says about social peace or justice. it can be trumped by the view that one's family or tribal connections are of first consideration. On the one hand there was a sense of freedom or nationhood; on the other hand there had to be a constant effort for social compromise, for keeping the ethnic groups in some sort of peaceable and productive relationship. When this effort broke down, the results were cataclysmic.

This tension between nationhood and tribalism was illustrated by an incident that happened in our home in 1972. Burundi was in civil unrest. People were dying by the thousands. One of our senior pastors used to come to our house for refuge when the army units were in the village rounding up "the enemy." (To the Tutsi government, the enemy was any educated Hutu or Hutu in leadership position.) The pastor had already lost a son and a son-in-law in the trouble, perhaps more. I said, "Pastor, don't you see that the country was better off in colonial days? At least there would not have been all this bloodshed."

The pastor's mouth flew open. "What are you talking about?" he said. "We may be having problems, but at least we are free!"

When independence approached in 1962 (1960 for Congo), the Belgians left the kingdom intact in Burundi because it related well to the Hutu majority. Being a democratic nation, Belgium could not accept leaving Rwanda in the hands of its very autocratic kingdom. Thus, when the Rwanda king died in 1959, the Belgian government helped leaders of the majority group to establish the Rwandan

Republic. The process was violent. Between 1959 and 1963, some 300,000 people were killed and as many fled to other countries in east Africa. At independence time Rwanda had a republic elected by the majority, while in Burundi there was still a kingdom. This kingdom was overthrown in 1967, and the country was declared the Republic of Burundi. It was led by a series of army commanders.

All the ensuing disturbances reported in the news during our time in Africa were influenced by the desire to maintain or seize power by opposing tribes. Everybody wanted to rule. Also, there were the continuing problems of heavy population, limited resources and very little industrialization.

In Burundi in 1965, the Hutu head of the national police force tried to stage a coup to take power for the majority. His effort was short-lived. The majority was always the Hutus and the minority was the Tutsis. Hutus used to make up 85 % of the population, Tutsis 14%, and pygmies 1%. The minority government saw their chance to eliminate the majority parliamentary deputies whom they feared. In that civil disturbance, 50,000 leaders and so-called enemies died.

In April 1972, a group of Royalists tried to stage a coup to re-establish the kingdom in Burundi. The Royalists were Tutsi offspring of the king. The other subgroup of Tutsis were the Bahima, who settled in an area called Bururi. The government reaction was violent. The Bahima asked the Royalists to work with them against the Hutus, and, in return, the Royalists would be absolved of their efforts to stage a coup and take over the government. The two groups worked together to kill the educated youth and leaders of any type in the Hutu tribe. The Hutu majority was advancing in commerce, education, even in government. 250,000 people died in two months. Many church leaders were killed as well as most of our school headmasters. Hutus were always upwardly mobile. The Tutsis' goal was to destroy Hutu leadership in all walks of life. Most of the students of Hutu origin in the high schools and universities were killed; amazingly those in our Mweya Bible Institute and Seminary were spared.

In 1973 there was a further mass killing of 50,000. Some Protestant and Catholic missionaries and leaders were instrumental in exposing the situation by informing press outside the country. Otherwise, the violence may have continued.

In March of 1993, because of international pressure to democratize, a Hutu president was elected and installed in Burundi. In October of that year he was brutally tortured and murdered. The Hutu majority group started revenge killings of the minority group, of whom some 20,000 died. Of course, the Tutsi government responded in kind. This time the majority group vowed they would not be "slaughtered like goats" as had happened in 1972. A ten-year civil war followed. Finally the Tutsi people were tired of their children in the army being killed by rebels. There were long discussions as to how to establish the peace. Former President Nelson Mandela from South Africa used his authority to broker the peace.

Burundi now has a constitutional government with equal representation from the two major groups in the armed forces. The president is a former rebel commander who found God in the heat of battle. That is the situation in Burundi at the time of this writing.

All this time Rwanda experienced ups and downs as a republic, with three different presidents serving from 1959 to 1994. In 1993, the Rwanda government got word of a plot being planned to assassinate the Hutu president, as had happened in Burundi. The government was determined to prepare for such an event. Secretly, the infamous *Interahamwe* was formed and trained to kill as many Tutsis as possible, in the event that their president should be assassinated. The *Interahamwe* were radical militant Hutu.

Meanwhile, a civil war had started in the early 1990's as the children of the Tutsi group that had fled between 1959 and 1963 made an effort to return. The rebels of the Rwanda Patriotic Front (RPF) were being helped by the Republic of Uganda. The first effort to invade the country was repulsed due to disunity among the rebel leaders. Two were actually killed. Then the RPF regrouped and slowly made their advance, cutting off the capital Kigali's power supply and transport channels.

Then on April 6, 1994, the situation exploded on the world scene. President Habyarimana and the president of Burundi were traveling together. They were coming from peace negotiations in Dar-es-Salaam, Tanzania. They should have been flying by daylight, but the opposition to the Rwanda government had delayed the proceedings so long (some say purposely) that the presidential plane was coming in by night. Two loud blasts were heard over the city and the presidential plane came down with its nose against the perimeter wall of the president's house near the airport. Both presidents were killed. There is a strong debate as to which group shot down the airplane. Eye-witness reports would accuse the RPF, but they strongly deny this. To admit such a deed would have been to incur international disfavor, especially since they were coming from a peace conference. In any case, chaos and mayhem erupted as the *Interahamwe* enacted their plan of killing as many Tutsis as possible. They also targeted moderate Hutus who had called for peace and dialogue. Some call this pogrom "genocide." If that word is used, then one would have to say that it was double genocide, due to the actions the RPF would later take. Before the mayhem ended, some 800,000 people had died. When the *Interahamwe* started killing people, the RPF decided they needed to react quickly to save as many lives as possible. They quickly took over the city of Kigali. Soon a huge migration was headed out of the city. These people were fearful of the RPF and had already seen vicious attacks.

The RPF quickly gained control of the whole country except for the three provinces at the southwest of the country. The French army advisors to the Rwanda government held their ground to protect the mass of civilians that were fleeing through that area. When many of them had fled over the border into Congo, the French left, but by this holding action, France may have saved hundreds of thousands of lives. (Of course, the French have earned the unending disfavor of the RPF government.) As the RPF army fanned out over the country, revenge killings broke out. This was kept hidden but there are plenty of sources to corroborate this statement. I have read news articles, talked to eye witnesses and visited the maimed and wounded in the Anglican hospital over the border in Tanzania. Probably as many people died in that action as died in the first wave of killings at the hands of the *Interahamwe*.

All was not dark. Heroic stories have spread of people helping their brothers in the opposing tribe. Others report being helped from an unknown source. God had intervened. During these times of trouble in both Rwanda and Burundi, we saw God's hand at work. In huge refugee camps on both sides of the country, our pastors went to work with their lay leaders to conduct services and to evangelize. People who had never understood the Gospel were ready to listen. This was probably true of various churches working in those camps, but the Free Methodists could report that, after two years, we had gained 20,000 members. As much as possible, the Free Methodist Church of the various camps conducted business just like they had back in their respective homelands. God was with them.

In the Burundian refugee camps, God was also at work. After the civil war started in October of 1993 in Burundi, thousands of refugees fled to Congo and Tanzania. In Tanzania, a group of 30 Free Methodists started worshiping in March of 1994. By November of 2002, that group had grown to well over 15,000. Choirs were organized. Compassion services, such as sponsorship of children in the refugee camps by people from other countries, were initiated. Primary schools were started. Women were doing special projects in their classes, like making baskets out of trashed plastic bags in which they had received food from the United Nations. They even had a Bible school for training pastors. A number of pastors were ordained in the camps. For many years, the Burundian church had been limited in reaching out to new provinces, thanks to an oppressive government. But in the camps we had refugees from all over the country. When they went home, they were challenged to start Free Methodist Churches in their home areas. Soon calls were coming in to the central office to receive and enfold these new church groups. Our Burundi church is now truly a national church.

Many times in the civil strife described above, the Africans were tempted to ask if God really loved them. We answer this way: it is Satan that doesn't like Africans. God wants to redeem them and give them new life.

Jesus said, "The thief comes only to steal and kill and destroy; I am come that they may have life, and have it to the full." John 10:10

Chapter 8

Free Methodist Education in Central Africa

All educated Africans in Burundi, Rwanda and Congo speak French or English. Before the genocide, not many English speakers could be found in those countries. After the invasion of Tutsis from Uganda, that changed. English is the official language in Uganda because its people were under British rule, like Kenya, before independence. After the genocide, teachers were required to teach English in the primary schools in Rwanda. (It was amusing to me to find out that one primary school teacher we know named her baby "Funny" because she liked the word and how it sounds.) In the past Congolese spoke French better than people in Burundi and Rwanda. I think that is not the case now.

Girls tend to drop out of school early to help with the farming and caring for the children. In the past by the time the class got to the eighth grade, there would only be a couple girls left. They learn to read in their own language. They sing and pray and read the Bible in the language of their heart (their first language). Even though the official papers were in French, the conversation would be in the language of the people. At some point in primary school, children in Burundi and Rwanda started to learn French. Before that, they had to learn to read in their native language. Congo primary school started French study much earlier.

Education for women in central Africa is a very difficult issue for three reasons. First of all, protein deficiency in childhood destroys their brains so that learning is a great challenge; it's a miracle they are even alive. Secondly, the tradition of Africa to feed grown men the best food, leaving whatever remains for the children and women, has been a curse. Thirdly, nobody in the world works as hard as a central African woman who lives outside the city. From the time she is able, as young as five or six years, she is carrying somebody's baby, most often her own brother or sister. She carries the water. She hunts for firewood to cook the food. She cultivates the garden with a seven-pound hoe. All the while she carries a baby.

Families were constantly being advised via radio to get their dishes off the ground and make a table to put their dishes on. Women were accustomed to doing everything in a squatting position or sitting on a little stool. It was the woman who ground the manioc (tapioca root) or grain with a mortar and pestle and stirred the flour into the boiling water on the fire to make their bread (*ugali* or *umutsima*).

The reason we built schools is because the government did not have enough schools for all the children. Christian Children's Fund really helped us in this endeavor. Wherever there were needs, that's where the mission tried to help.

The mission as such no longer exists in places in Africawhere there is a Free Methodist general conference.

Anything done in Africa now is and should be solely through the African church leadership.

From the beginning Free Methodists prioritized education. When there were enough African teachers to teach the elementary/primary schools, high schools were started. Missionaries were the directors of those schools until there were enough educated Africans to direct and teach in them. Free Methodists have invested heavily in educating leaders from the beginning. The same goes for pastoral training.

The schools that the church started were called non-subsidized schools, because the government gave us no money to pay the teachers in those schools. The curriculum, the calendar, and the schedule were the same as government schools. We use the term secondary school all the time in Africa when we mean high school. It is called *ecole secondaire* in French too.

The school we started the year we lived at Kibogora in Rwanda was for children of school age who were not in school. Their parents could not afford the school fees or the children had difficulty learning and were dropouts at an early age. It was such a stigma not to be in school with others their age that I saw this as a great need to be met. Because I had worked with Christian Children's Fund from Denmark in Burundi, they readily accepted to continue helping in Rwanda. After we left, the local government took over the sponsorship of that school with CCF.

The government exam at the end of primary school determined the future of every child. If they passed, they went on to high school. If they did not, it was the end of their schooling until technical schools were started to teach trades. The Home Economics school of Muyebe, Burundi for girls was already in existence when we got there. Often

Bible Institutes for training pastors were for people who had not passed the government exams. That changed in the years we lived at Mweya. That was when Mweya Bible Institute started teaching in French. Before that teaching had been in the local language and in English, because most commentaries and holiness literature were in English. Missionaries wanted the students to know the Bible in the language of their hearts. There was a definite push to introduce French so that the graduates of the Bible Institute who would become pastors and leaders in their communities could communicate fluently with government leaders. It was a matter of prestige. The first girls to be accepted in the Bible Institute came while we were there.

Free Methodists asked for land near the city of Kigali in Rwanda for the building of a university before the rampage of 1994. Expropriation of land for the university was just beginning when the genocide started. It was to be a university sponsored by the Central Africa Area Fellowship of the Free Methodist World Fellowship.

The bishops of our Free Methodist Church were evacuated to Kenya during the ongoing conflict that affected not only Rwanda, but also Burundi and Congo. At that time, Jim, along with the bishops, began planning to start the university in Kenya. The Karen Free Methodist Church was across the street from the Nairobi Evangelical Graduate School of Theology where we were living and I was working. Right beside that plot of land we bought for the church was a bar and whore house. Neighbors were distressed because of the bad effects the bar and the whore house were having on their young people. The bar owner was happy to have the church built there, thinking that the church attendees would visit the bar after worship service. That did not happen. Instead, the business at the bar so decreased that the bar was closed. So we rented the building to start the university there. Bishop Elie Buconyori, Jim, and I walked throughout all the building and prayed in every room for every evil spirit to be gone and for Jesus Christ to be exalted. Soon the government let us know that we had to own 50 acres of land to build a university in order to be accredited. We bought the 50 acres of land outside the city of Nairobi. Greenville College in Illinois was to give the diplomas, but, of course, the Kenya government did not like that. Then the government said we had to build the buildings on the 50 acres before we could start classes. Bishop Elie was in favorable relationship with government leaders in Burundi. The entire school, after just a few years of existence in Kenya, was packed up and hauled by truck over to Burundi where it has flourished to this day.

Before it came into existence, Hope Africa University was part of long-range planning and efforts of Central Africa Area Fellowship for many years. It is a Free Methodist university, not a mission university—but solely under the Free Methodist Church in central Africa, although Free Methodists from the U.S. contribute heavily both in personnel and in finances. It is a liberal arts university and now has medical training. Most of the professors are Africans who have been trained in other schools. However, personnel from the U.S. go out regularly to teach. Recently the first U.S. personnel have gone on more permanent assignment to live and teach in the medical school. Before, mainly retired medical personnel from the U.S. went to teach in the medical school.

Since the current leaders in Rwanda are from Uganda and studied English and not French, both languages are being taught in Rwanda. Hope Africa University is teaching both in English and in French, depending on the language of the professor.

More than 5000 students are currently enrolled in Hope Africa University in Burundi. They are from both tribes. I am sure this will make a difference in the quality of teachers in primary and high schools, and the quality of life for the general public.

Dr. Doane Bonney, Director of Free Methodist World Mission, and my husband Jim. Between them stand the first African Free Methodist bishops in Burundi (Noah Nzeyimana), in Congo (Jason Mzuri) now deceased, and in Rwanda (Aaron Ruhumuriza) now deceased

My last class at NEGST who graduated in 2004

Chapter 9

M a r i y a

Isaiah 11:16 . . . a little child shall lead them.

We lived for ten years (1984-1994) in a university town called Butare in the tiny country of Rwanda in Africa, a country about the size of the state of Maryland. It was home to the Rwanda National University, supported mainly by French Canadians. To me, Butare was the most beautiful town in Africa. The main street of the town is lined with jacaranda trees that produce fragrant lavender flowers every year. The market place has a cement floor and a good roof overhead; different from any other market I ever saw in Africa. French Canadians supported the university and regularly sent professors to teach there. The support included building new houses for their professors every couple years.

We were sent by the Rwanda Free Methodist Church to Butare to live. Our assignment was to help an African pastor start a Free Methodist Church in that town. There was also a theological school for the training of pastors in that town. We were asked to teach in the theological school. Several different denominations worked together in that school, which made it stronger. Our Bishop, Aaron Ruhumuriza, had specifically chosen people who had done well in high school to be sent to the theological school. He was getting them ready as candidates that would be sent out to the towns in the different townships (prefectures) as church planters. On weekends we would take them out with us in gospel teams and work in the surrounding villages.

One Sunday, we went to a very poor church on a hillside. Rain was pouring. It was rainy season. The roof was just grass—it wasn't adequate—so the rain was coming right through the grass roof. There was no floor; just dirt, and the walls were made of mud plastered on sticks. People sat in little groups where the rain wasn't dripping as much. Somebody brought a bench for the men from the theological school and for us to sit on up in front. Then they laid grass mats around us, and the children sat on those grass mats. There were 27 little children. They were right up against us so that they were touching us. They were just crowded in. 27 little children. I counted that 21 of those 27 children had the symptoms of *kwashiorkor* (a protein deficiency disease) that would make their black hair turn orange and straight instead of black and kinky. The children were very puffy—a puffy face and puffy arms and legs and a big stomach. They were lethargic and quiet. Ordinarily, no child in an advanced stage of the disease ever reaches adulthood. The men that went with us from the theological school said they had never seen that many sick children in one place.

Those people had all walked to that little church they had built themselves. We were there early and watched the people come in. One little girl was sicker than anybody else. She was six years old but was too weak to walk and so her mother had carried her in a cloth on her back. She put the child on a mat with the other children. Those children just sat there the whole time we were in that service, about three hours. No one ever had to tell those kids to be quiet. They didn't have energy to do anything. They just sat there. But I saw that Mariya, the one brought on her mother's back, was more ill than any of the other children. I went to her mother after church and I said, "You know, you need to get your little child to the doctor. She is very ill."

She said "Well, I've been praying about it."

I said "No, you have to do more than pray about it, you have to get her to the doctor, to the hospital." She kind of hem-hawed, and I said, "Okay, this is what I'll do. I'll come out here at 9 o'clock tomorrow morning. I'll pick you up with your little girl and I'll take her to the hospital. I'll help you get her there."

The hospital had a *kwashiorkor* clinic where mothers could go with their sick children and stay. The nurses would teach the mothers how to feed them nutritiously. Mariya was in that hospital for six months. Her mother and her teenage sister would take turns staying with her. All the time they were taught how to feed her nutritiously. Afterwards the mother told me, "I never knew it was my responsibility to feed my children a good diet until I went to that hospital. I thought that if a child lived, it was God's will. If they died, it was God's will. I never realized till then that it was my responsibility." It was hard for me to understand how a mother's heart could not feel responsible to care for her child properly. Lack of knowledge is a horrible thing.

Anyway, Mariya got well, and she went back to school. Miracle of miracles, her mind was not damaged. Usually children are unable to learn after they've had that disease. She finished the next school year at the top of her class—the smartest one in her class. The teacher was amazed.

Mariya got this idea—she should do something to repay us for all we had done to help her. She went to her mother one day and said, "Now, I know that we're poor, and there's nothing I could give to the Kirkpatricks to repay them for helping me. But there is something that I can *do*. I feel like God wants me to get up early in the morning before I go to school every day and pray for them." She asked her teenage sister and her mother if they would get up and pray with her. The teenage sister said, "That's not the time to pray; that's the time to sleep." But Mariya followed through on her commitment.

Mariya would get up before it was light. Every morning they would do this—the mother and her little girl would get up and pray before it was time for her to go to school. One day, the mother walked to our house. Jim said it was about a two and a half hour walk for her to get to our house in town. She said, "While Mariya was praying this morning, she said, 'Mama, I see the Kirkpatricks up in the air on a big, black bird, and the bird falls into a deep, dark hole.'"

The mother said, "I know Mariya doesn't know much about airplanes but that told me that you're going on a trip and you're going to have trouble. I called the church people all together. We prayed and prayed until we felt that God had heard our prayer, and you would be okay. I came to tell you what happened. Now I want to know, are you going to make a trip?"

"Yes!" I said, "We're leaving today! We're going to Kinshasa on the other side of Congo."

She patted me and said, "You're going to be okay. We've prayed for you, God's going to take care of you."

To get to Congo from there, we drove through the rain forest and over to Kibogora to the mission hospital. Jim wanted to stop there on the way. When we stopped our car, these church women, African women from Kibogora, came and surrounded our car. They said, "We've come from a prayer meeting and God has shown us that you're going to have trouble on this trip. We have prayed for you that you're going to be okay."

I looked at Jim, and I said, "Well if TWO groups of people have had this feeling, maybe we should turn around and go home and not make this trip."

Jim said, "No, with these two groups of people praying for us we will be okay." We went to Bukavu, right across the border from Rwanda, and got on a little plane and flew up to Goma, and got on a big plane to go across Congo. Then we'd go on from there to Cameroon and Nigeria.

We boarded that big airplane, a cast-off European or American plane: that's what African planes were. The plane didn't sound healthy at all. We got to Kisangani. We short-landed—disembarked before our planned destination—on the airstrip. There was no place for us to go. The passengers just got off. We stood around in the sun for an hour and a half while they worked on the generator for the electrical system on that airplane. Then we got back on, and we arrived safely in Kinshasa. We spent our month there in west Africa and came home safely. I thanked God for people that pray for us like Mariya, my prayer partner in Africa.

We visited all the time back and forth because Mariya liked us. She was about eight or nine years old at that time. Six months later it was time to go again to west Africa. We would spend a month over there teaching pastors. When we were loading the car, I said to Jim, "Whew! I'm glad Mariya's mother didn't come in today—that means we're going to have a safe trip."

There was always a lot of excitement in Kinshasa that had nothing to do with Mariya. One morning very early, we prepared to head home. We'd had a safe trip to west Africa and, after a month, it was about 5:30 in the morning that we had to go to the airport to board our plane. To get to the airport we went in a taxi. Young men would circle around our car or taxi when they'd see white people and they would want to carry our suitcases. They'd tell us, "Oh, there's a new law—you have to have help getting your visa stamped," They would want us to pay them. If a person weren't careful, they would abscond with your passport, ticket or suitcase and you would never see them again. We just never allowed anybody to do that—we always had friends from the church with us anyway. They would help us. Somebody in this crowd of people came around to "help" us; calling and making all kinds of commotion. Somebody reached over Jim's shoulder and pulled his pen out of his pocket. Quick as a flash, Jim had that man on the ground! It was just a reflex. He got his pen back. From then until we boarded that airplane, no heckler bothered us. They would say, "Watch out for that old, white man! He's really strong!"

We got on the plane, and we were flying for about half an hour. Jim said, "Something's funny about this. The sun is coming up on the wrong side of the plane for us to be going to Bukavu."

Pretty soon the pilot said, "Due to technical difficulties, we are returning to Kinshasa." It was weird how passengers got hysterical. Some people got sick and some were crying and praying out loud to God and to Allah. The attendants were busy trying to comfort people. It was quite an experience.

I asked Jim, "Are you scared? Are you afraid?"

He answered, "No, I have peace." I started praying. And I couldn't figure out if I had peace or not. But I hoped I did.

117

I started praying that if we died, God would do something special to comfort our children and our parents. That gave me a sense of peace that God would do something special for them. We got back to the airport and sat, waiting for them to get the plane repaired. Late in the afternoon, they finally let us get back on the plane, and we started our trip to go to Bukavu. We had a safe trip. When we got to Bukavu, it was too late to cross the border back home to Rwanda. The border closed at 6 p.m. We stayed the night in Bukavu with Free Methodist missionaries Bud and Lois Ansted. When we got home at about 9 the next morning, guess who was waiting at our door? Mariya's mother. She said, "I came to your house yesterday and you weren't home. We had a prayer meeting for you, because Mariya told us that you were going to have trouble. The church people gathered all together to pray for you. I just felt so bad that you weren't here yesterday so that I could tell you that God was going to take care of you. Then I thought, 'Well, it doesn't matter whether they know or not. The important thing is that God knows! He has answered our prayer, and he's going to take care of them.'"

I told her then, about our trip. She was so happy that God was using them to pray for us. I was happy, too. We've had people in the States that God has impressed to pray for us, but Mariya was a faithful prayer partner all the time—the rest of those years that we were in Butare. I never heard from her again after the massacre of 1994. Having a friend like Mariya was a wonderful gift.

Mariya and her mother

Chapter 10

The Beggar

I want to tell you a story about when we lived at Mweya, before the war of 1972. At Mweya we lived in the house that Jim's dad and older brother, Don, built. It was the first permanent home that Jim's family had in Africa.

We went back to Africa in July 1969 after home assignment. We celebrated Len's first birthday in that house. Jim's mom and dad were there for the birthday party. We had just arrived; we didn't even have our furniture moved up from Bujumbura, the capital, yet. We were just camping until we could get our house settled. Now, this big house that Jim's dad had built and we lived in was in the center of the mission station. On this mission station they had a printing press, a Bible Institute and a missionary children's school. The Bible Institute was a school to train pastors at the high school level. The Free Methodists, the WGM, and the Friends church ran it together, and we had many missionaries living on the station. The children would attend the missionary children's school. We also had a dormitory for expatriate children from other places in Burundi to stay.

Even though it was mostly missionary children, we did have children whose parents were not missionaries that came there to school. Often we had visitors from other places. The governor would visit. Church leaders from other places would have meetings there. We had a large student body in the Bible Institute; there must have been around 100 students at that time. There was a lot going on at that mission station. We also had a Free Methodist Church just over the hill from our house, which was well attended.

During this time, there was a couple attending the church who were recently married. While their baby, their first child, was on the way, the father died. When the baby was born, they named him "The one who was left behind." That's what they call babies who are born after the father dies "*Mizigaro.*" This child who was left behind was very deformed in his legs and feet and couldn't walk. He just sat on the ground and pulled himself along with a stick. He was mentally challenged but kind. Life was very difficult for his mother. Her husband's family put her out. They disowned her. They may have disowned her because they considered her bad luck or because they wanted the land that had been given to her husband. Here she was, a homeless widow with a crippled, mentally challenged child. It was very sad. She did what homeless people do: she begged every day and so did her son as he grew.

The missionaries at Mweya went together and bought an acre of land and built a house for her on this land. They gave her a hoe and things that were necessary, a bed, pots, pans and dishes. She had become a beggar. She didn't know what else to do. She would just stay wherever anybody would let her stay overnight before she had her own house. Every day she made her way around to all the missionaries' houses to beg—for sugar, for milk, for clothes, for a blanket, for something different at every house. And she was VERY unkempt. Dirty. Stinky. And she never went to the back door like beggars usually do; she always went to the front door of the house—so people could see what she was doing. She wanted to be noticed. She needed love. It seemed like the more people tried to help her, the more she expected from everybody. It was a strange problem. I got so tired of her.

One day, 8 in the morning, I was going down to the school to teach. In my mind I thought, "I'm going to ignore that woman today; I'm tired of her always being here at the door, as part of the scenery. Maybe if I ignore her, because we've done all we know to do for her, maybe she'll just go away and quit begging. We won't give her anything."

I started out the door with my books to go down to the school, and a voice came in my head, strongly, and the voice said, "MARTHA, I love her just as much as I love you." I felt as though I was choking. It was like a shock that this came to me. And I knew I could not go down to school without doing something for that woman. Margi, our daughter, remembers I gave her cabbage. I think I gave her bread. I don't know. I don't remember what I gave her. I went back into the house and wrapped it up, which was the custom, and took it to the woman. I said, "I want to tell you something. Jesus loves you. And so do I." I'll never forget how her face changed when I said that. All at once this whiney, begging woman's face changed into a smiling face. It was as though, in my doing that, a realization came to her that she was accepted and loved. I don't know if she changed or I changed. I don't remember her coming to the door after that. I never again felt annoyed by her. More than that, it was life-changing for me. It was as though I woke up to realize everyone is on the same level in God's eyes. There are no favorites. You can achieve all you want in this world but it doesn't change how much God loves the people that don't achieve, that can't achieve. The important truth to get across to everybody is that Jesus loves them.

. . . . that whoever believes in him should not perish, but have everlasting life. John 3:16

Chapter 11

God Takes Care of Us

We had many interesting and varied experiences in our second term in Burundi, when the genocide of 1972 happened.

We lived at Mweya, nicknamed Windy Hill. On Mweya's hill we had a Bible institute for training pastors, a printing press, and a missionary children's school, all on the same station. Missionaries and African personnel worked in these schools and the printing press. Students from central Africa in the Bible institute and the missionary children's school were also on campus. In 1970, a wonderful revival came to Windy Hill. People confessed their sins and were filled with the Holy Spirit. It was life-changing for many. The same movement of the Holy Spirit happened in other schools in Rwanda and Burundi. Many of the Bible institute students were Free Methodist boys, including the man who is now Bishop Elie Buconyori. After that special moving of God on the campus, the students went out during vacation to different churches, telling what wonderful things had happened. People needed to get saved. They needed to surrender all and be filled with the Spirit of God. Later, when the slaughter came in 1972, those students said, "God visited us in a special way in 1970, to get people ready to go to heaven."

During the genocide that came in 1972, soldiers went around to high schools, which were the academic level of our Bible institute. They would call the names of the students that were in the wrong tribe, because they didn't want them to be educated. They would load them up on trucks and take them out to mass graves already prepared. Some of them they shot, but most of the students they just hit on the back of the head with clubs. Then they would throw them into mass graves.

Our school was the only school in the country that was not touched. The village elder, the chief, and Jim were really good friends. The chief kept telling Jim, "I don't want any blood on my hands in the judgment. Nobody in my area that I'm responsible for is going to die." The only student we lost in the school was one boy named Niyonzima, who was worried about his parents. Jim and I can still see him in our mind's eye. He slipped home to check on them not far from the school, and he dropped his identity card in the path. The military found it and came to the school. Jim had gone to the capital, Bujumbura, that day to hand over legal documents to the assistant church legal representative, because our legal representative had been taken and not heard from again. The soldiers came to our house and asked for the student. I could not think fast enough to know what to do, so I went down to the school, praying all the way, to Jim's assistant, Willard Ferguson, who was teaching that hour and told him what the soldiers wanted. Would you believe it, Niyonzima was sitting right there in Willard's class? They took him out of class, put him in their vehicle, and took him away. No farewell, never heard of again. No words can express the shock, the grief, of Willard and me at that moment. To lose one student was one too many. All the rest of the students were safe. We had a curfew—students had to be in the dorm from 6 in the evening to 6 in the morning. As director of the Bible institute, Jim was very strict in an effort to care for them.

We had a brand new Volkswagen Combi, a van to haul people in. The first trip it made was to take a gospel team out to a church on Sunday, the day the massacre began. We did not know it was going to start. The soldiers took those students, and also the driver, who was Jim's assistant. They locked them up overnight. They released the students the next day. The students walked 25 miles back to school and told us that our brand new van had been impounded, and the military was holding Jim's assistant. Jim thought, "What can I do so that I can get that man released and get the vehicle released?" He convinced someone to drive him to Muyebe (the oldest Free Methodist Church in Burundi), which was on the way to where the man and the car were being held. Jim asked the missionary there to drive him to the van and then go home leaving him at the government office. When he got to the government office he said, "I've come to pick up my van and to get my assistant released. I really need him in the school." It took a long discussion but they finally released the van and his assistant. They released the assistant, Joel Masambiro, on one condition: that he would report to them the next morning. Jim took Joel home where he stayed the night with his wife and reported to the government office the next morning. We never heard from him again. They killed him. That may have been one of the greatest disappointments for us in Africa. Back at Mweya we had special and long prayers for Joel. I thought for sure it was going to be a repeat of Acts 12 and, like Peter, our Joel would be returned to us. It was not to be.

Nobody could replace Joel in our lives. He had been a business man before he started working with us at Mweya. He was known in the community as an honest, straightforward man. He had built a fine house for his family at Rwintare. We were their neighbors our first term. He built another house for his family there at Mweya. Joel was one in a million. We trusted him. He was absolutely reliable, always on time or early. He was careful with his reports. He had charge of the food and the students in the dormitory.

Once the students went on strike because the water pump was broken down. That meant that water had to be carried from the source in the valley to the school. They were asked to carry their own water for bathing and washing their clothes. They refused to do it. Food for the evening meal was prepared and served as usual, but they did not come to eat. Jim asked Joel, "What shall we do?"

Joel said, "Leave the food on the tables. Hunger is a good policeman. They will show up. They will eat, and they will carry water. Don't give in." It happened just as Joel said. By morning the food was all gone and cooperation returned.

Joel's wife was a saint. Her name was Veronica. Veronica was humble and patient. They reared their children well. The last we knew their son was working in the bishop's office. Veronica as a widow gave a victorious witness in the local Mweya church one Sunday morning. That afternoon as she stood in the doorway of their home, lightning struck her and killed her. Their children were left as orphans.

Anyway, this genocide went on! 1972, 1973, this slaughter. They killed thousands of people. Jim saw some of them being killed—but he will never say anything about it. He told me about it once and told me never to bring it up again. He said, "We'll never talk about this." And we never have. An amazing perspective is that the missionary children in the boarding school were unaware of what was going on. Our own children said they did not know until we came home to the U.S. and they heard us tell some stories. We know God watched over our children.

For electricity at Mweya we used a diesel generator. We didn't have electricity throughout the country. We would just have electricity from 6 to 9 in the evening. At 9 p.m. the generator would shut down. Everything would be quiet and dark. One night a military truck rolled onto the station and parked at our house just after 9 p.m. We peeked out the window and saw the soldiers surround our house. Remember, this is a big mission station with lots of missionaries there but they surrounded *our* house. Jim asked me, "Should I go to the door?" and I said "NO! Not unless they knock." They never knocked. I don't know how many trips they made around the house. Our dog never barked once, which was unusual for him. I don't know if they gave him meat to eat or what made him be quiet, but he never made a noise. After a while, they got back into the truck and left. They went back and reported to the governor, "There's nothing going on at that mission station. Everything's quiet. That director is in his house, it's all dark. Everything's quiet. Those people are doing right." So nothing came of that. (That was reported to us by a soldier.)

*   *   *

From 1960 to 1962, when we were in school at Asbury in Wilmore, Kentucky, an elderly Methodist evangelist named Dr. Warren C. McIntyre asked the dean of women if I could stay with his invalid wife when he went away in meetings in churches. He paid me for doing this. I fed her and helped her dress before I went to school each morning. I also worked in the registrar's office until class started and after class in the afternoon. I did that for a year. When Jim and I were engaged to be married, I said to the evangelist, "I'm not going to be able to continue this; we're getting married."

He said, "You come and let me show you what I have." He took me upstairs, and showed me the cutest little apartment. It had not been used for 20 years because his wife Luvena couldn't stand the noise of anybody upstairs but she liked me. He said, "If you'll stay in this apartment, and stay with Luvena downstairs whenever I'm away in meetings, I will give you room and board." She died while we were there, but he continued to give us free room and board till we left.

Well, here we were in Africa in 1972 in these difficult days, and the evangelist was too frail to travel and have meetings in churches. He wrote to the Free Methodists, to the Wesleyans, to World Gospel Mission, and to OMS, and asked for the names of all their missionaries. He prayed for all of them every day. I still have the paper where he wrote about the incident in *God's Revivalist* (The magazine from God's Bible School in Cincinnati, Ohio). Once, while he was praying for us in this group of missionaries, he said, he *saw* soldiers carrying our furniture out of our house during his prayer time and the soldiers were harassing us. He prayed and prayed and prayed that God would spare our lives and this would not happen to us. It was the *very* day that these soldiers were around our house.

Chapter 12

HELENE

In 1975 we lived in Bujumbura, the capital of Burundi, in the center of the city in a house owned by Radio CORDAC. Jim was helping to start churches outside Bujumbura. You have to know that Bujumbura was in the valley. It was a long valley from Tanzania up to Rwanda; part of the Great Rift system. There are several branches of the Rift Valley, but they are all interconnected. The Rift Valley goes clear up to northern Israel. The Zambezi River flows into the Rift Valley. They raise coffee and cotton there. Immediately after leaving the city, we would climb up into the mountains where the antenna site was for the radio station. Mweya and all those other places were up in the mountains.

When the Belgian colonists were ready to turn the government over to the Africans, they built a complex in the capital city of Bujumbura in Burundi for the Catholics. The complex included a school and a church with offices and apartments for people to live in. They also did that for the Protestants. The Alliance of Protestant Churches voted to give their complex to the Free Methodists. In our first term, we lived in one of those apartments. Then they turned those apartments over to the leaders of the church, who were Africans, after independence. That's why we rented a house in the center of the city.

There were many Tutsi refugees in Burundi from Rwanda in those years. Some lived near our church in Ngagara, the Bujumbura suburb. Some lived in northeast Burundi not far from Murore. Kirk, Jim's dad, had a special concern for them. He got scholarships for some to study to be pastors. He helped with the building of churches.

Wherever we lived I would always have classes for women—teaching them to sew; to cook; to care for their babies and care for their personal hygiene needs. At the end of the class we would have a devotional time, Bible study and prayer, with all the women. African women are very courteous. They might come late to the sewing class but they would never leave until it was time to leave. I learned that's when you have your Bible study—at the end. When I was having class where our church was, in a suburb called Ngagara, a woman came to my class that was a zealous Christian. She was friendly in helping other women; urging them to become Christians. She was an answer to my prayers to be an influence on other African women. I could never get her to tell me from where she came. One day I asked other women in the church. This is the story I garnered:

Helene was from Rwanda, the country to the north. She had six children; had lived up there in a nice house. Her husband was a nurse. The Anglicans and the Free Methodists had regular training for medical personnel. Kibogora, the Free Methodist mission, even had a medical school for training medical assistants. They would be accredited by the government. The government also had medical training. We never knew Helene and her husband in Rwanda. I only met her as a widow in Bujumbura, Burundi. Helene and her family were Anglicans. They were an educated family. By that I mean that Helene could read well. Her children went to secondary school. When the Belgians granted independence and enabled the Hutus to govern in Rwanda in 1959, it was a sad day for people like Helene. They had money and they were of the Tutsi tribe. One day, soldiers came to their house; and tied up her husband inside the house and demanded that Helene give them the family's life savings, which was about $5,000 (a lot of money). Helene's husband might have been making $3 a day or $5 if he was good at his profession. We didn't know him. They poured gasoline on the house. Helene begged to die with him. They refused for her to be in the house with him. They made her and the children stand there while they torched the house and burned her house down; burned him alive in that house. They told her, "We want you to get out of here. We don't ever want to see your face again. We want you to leave." So she walked from her home in Rwanda to the Burundi border. She knelt at the border with her children and promised God that she would never complain and she would never ask anyone for money. She told me of her promise after I told her that I had found out about how she arrived among us. She never did ask for help. She was a victorious Christian.

One day I said to Helene, "Now that I know your story, isn't there something I could do to help you?"

She said "Oh, no! I promised I would never complain; I would never ask anybody for anything. I can't ask you for anything. But I can tell you things that God has done to help me."

She told about her son walking to high school every day. He would stay at school all day without eating and come home at night. A merchant, who had a store, saw him passing the store every day on his way to high school. He stopped him, and talked to him, just got to know him. When he found out that he wasn't eating all day long, the merchant asked him to come and have lunch at his house every day during lunch break. As he got to know the family, he had this boy stay in his home close to the school during the school days and go back to his house on weekends because it was too far for him to get to the school from home. That's what he did. Helene said, "See? That's how God has taken care of us all the way."

We went up-country to Mweya to get our children once a month to spend a weekend with us in the city where we lived. Up-country means that, when you leave the valley from Bujumbura, you climb a mile in altitude in an hour to Nyakarago. The altitude at Mweya, where the Bible Institute and missionary children's school were, is 5800 feet. As we passed where they made charcoal, between the missionary children's school and Bujumbura, we stopped and bought a big bag of charcoal to give Helene. She made bread using a barrel for an oven with racks in it and a charcoal fire beneath it. She baked her bread and sold it at the market to make a living. People liked her bread. She had no problem selling it. She would probably make buns most often.

One day she came to the women's class as happy as could be. She said, "I have to tell you this story of what happened to me last night. Yesterday morning, a beggar came to the door." She gave that beggar the last 50 francs she had. I don't remember the exact exchange rate but 50 francs would be comparable to 50 cents. As soon as she gave it away, she felt so awful, so guilty. She had given her last bit of money to a beggar that she did not know and she had six children for whom she was responsible. She said, "I'm giving my money to somebody I don't even know! I thought I was doing what God wanted me to do." She said that all day long she vacillated in her thoughts between feeling guilty that she had given her last bit of money to a beggar, and feeling that she really had done what God wanted her to do.

That night she read the Bible and prayed with her children. They had gone to bed and there was a knock at the door. She was afraid that it was a thief or somebody coming to bother her. She didn't want to open the door; it was dark. The person persisted, continued knocking. Finally she opened the door just a crack and a man stuck his hand in the door with a 1000 franc note. That would be comparable to 10 dollars. He said in the dark, "Take this. I don't know why I have to give it to you, but I want a good night's sleep. I know that if I do not give this to you, I'm not going to get any sleep. Something impressed me that I'm supposed to give this to you." She received it with thanks.

Helene told the women the next day, "I know that if I had not given that 50 francs to that beggar in the morning, I would have never received that thousand francs at night."

That's the kind of person that Helene was. She was remarkable. In the reality of her faith in Christ and the joy of living in spite of the horrible things that had happened to her, God made her a wonderful blessing in the neighborhood, in the church, in Burundi. She kept her promise that she would never complain; never ask anybody for anything. When we left Africa, she was elderly. Her children were intelligent and had gone on to higher education. She was a loyal Christian and her children turned out well.

To comfort all who mourn, and provide for those who grieve in Zion—to bestow on them a crown of beauty instead of ashes, the oil of gladness instead of mourning, and a garment of praise instead of despair. They will be called oaks of righteousness, a planting of the Lord for the display of his splendor. Isaiah 61:3

Chapter 13

Jim's Illness

I want to tell you about how God answered prayer. We had been in Africa about four months in 1965. A missionary nurse, Doris Moore, lived on Kibuye station and we were there. And that was it—we were the only missionaries. Everybody else was African. I could not speak the local language yet. A hospital was on the mission station, but we didn't have a doctor at that time. Jim had become very sick. In those days we communicated by radio with other mission stations. A doctor was telling Nurse Doris over the radio what medicine to give Jim. They gave him a malaria cure, but he remained ill. His fever was high. He was delirious some of the time. And he wasn't getting any better.

Doris put a mattress in the back of the old station wagon. Africans carried Jim out and laid him on the mattress. He was out of his head with fever. Beth was three and a half years old and Margi was two years. We all got in the car with Doris and went to Murore hospital over bumpy roads. It was about three hours away. Doctor John Brose was the doctor. He received Jim right away and did tests. Jim had malaria and strep throat. They decided he also had the flu. In the night, the bed would shake because he was shivering and had fever. I thought for sure I was going to bury him in Africa because of the extent of his illness and how long it lasted. We stayed in a nurse's house at Murore. At 2 a.m. I awakened the nurse and said I didn't know what to do to help him. She got the doctor. By now the doctor knew that he had strep throat. When Jim heard this man's voice, Jim said, "When I had strep throat in Michigan, the doctor gave me Erythromycin." The doctor said, "I can't believe it! This week I got that medicine in the pharmacy for the first time ever!" It was an antibiotic. Because the doctor didn't have any adult aspirin, he gave Jim 12 baby aspirin every three hours to get his fever down along with the Erythromycin. Jim started to improve. He lost 25 pounds and was out of commission for more than a month. He couldn't study, he couldn't do anything because he was so weak.

When we finally got back to Kibuye where we lived, our mail was waiting for us. There was a letter from a woman in Michigan who had been in our church that we pastored for two years before going to Africa. She said, "Tell me! How is Virgil?" "I have felt so concerned for him—I have been praying and praying for his health. There must be something wrong." Isn't that strange and good? God heard her prayers and delivered an antibiotic to the hospital at just the right time.

Chapter 14

The Faith of a Child

In 1972, there was a horrible massacre in Burundi. There was a great loss of potential leaders. All the smart children of one tribe were killed off. The military would back a truck up to a school, head inside, name the students of the opposite tribe, and make them get in the truck. Then they would take them to big open graves they had prepared. There they would either shoot them or club them in the head and toss them into the grave. A very few would pretend they were dead, somehow survive, and escape the grave. Most of them were buried in those graves.

One of our students was a spy. When we had faculty meetings or missionary prayer meetings we would find him squatting in the bushes beneath the window, which we opened when the weather was nice. He would listen to everything we said. He'd make up stories and report on us to the government authorities in the local town, Gitega. We knew it was happening but we just continued to pray. We didn't know what else to do. One night a truckload of soldiers came to the mission station, right after we turned off the electricity. They marched around our house. I can still hear them marching. They marched and marched. Our dog didn't bark . . . .

*   *   *

When Doris Ellen, our niece, was born in Burundi, she was born at night in the capital city. Her mother had a military ambulance and a military escort to the hospital because it was during curfew. Tim, her dad, was busy trying to keep the radio station going. It was a difficult time. When Doris Ellen was six weeks old, we had permission to travel to see her. Missionaries up-country had given us gifts for baby Doris. We had everything packed and were in the car with our permission to travel. I don't know how long it had been since we had been away from the mission station, but it had been a long time. When we got to the military camp, which might have been three or four miles from where we lived, there were barriers with soldiers at the barriers. They had sticks across the road as a checkpoint. They examined everything in our car and made sure that our pass was up to date, etc. When we got to the one at the military camp and they found out we were going to Bujumbura, they said, "You are not going!" We didn't know why, but they just stood there and tore up Jim's permission to travel right next to the car. We felt intimidated because it wasn't just one soldier; it was a group of soldiers with their guns.

Jim said, "This permission to travel isn't just for Bujumbura, I have places that I'm responsible for. I have to visit my pastors. I have to visit those churches!" All of the places were up-country in the mountains. The soldiers were gruff, and they told him to come with them. I didn't know whether they were gruff because he had made them aggravated, or if this was just to show that they were more powerful. They took him, escorted him into the military camp and left the children and me sitting in the car by the side of the road. I kept wondering what was going on in there. Were they being kind to my husband? Len, who was four years old, patted me on the shoulder and said, "Mom, it's okay. If anything happens to Dad in there, Jesus will just say 'Come on up, Uncle Jim!' And he'll go up."

Jim says he was there about 20 minutes but it seemed a lot longer than 20 minutes to us. He came back out. When he was released, he did *not* have permission for us to go to the capital, so we turned around and went back home.

It was a while longer before we ever saw Doris. They did give Jim permission to travel to the up-country churches that he was working with. We found out later that there was a special envoy from the U.N. that was in Bujumbura at the time. The soldiers did not want the U.N. people to have any contact with people from up country because they did not want the U.N. to know what was happening: that students in high schools were being slaughtered and buried in mass graves, that upstanding members of the community were being taken, never to be seen again. They did not want the U.N. to know that the up-country prisons were full of people who had been arrested just because they were of the wrong tribe.

Chapter 15

Philip's Birth and
My Sickness

Dear Philip,

I want to tell you about why it's important . . . why it's significant to me that you are the one who is listening to my stories and wanting to write them down.

We had planned for months that, when you were born in April, 1990, I would travel to the U.S. to be with your mom. We were on home assignment and went back to Africa for a short time during the year because Grandpa was area director and I was coordinator for central Africa for International Child Care Ministries (ICCM). The people from Washington who were building the church in the rain forest stayed in our house during that year.

First, we traveled across Africa on our way to the states. I was visiting sponsored children from Rwanda to Nigeria. (The Free Methodists have a program called International Child Care Ministries. Originally people in the U.S. would sponsor pastors' children and orphans in poor countries who were in the Free Methodist Church. Then they sponsored schools. The program is similar to World Vision and Compassion International. Alton Gould, the founder, a missionary in Hong Kong, said, "Why shouldn't Free Methodists be able to sponsor their own in other countries?" So ICCM came into being.)

The last place I went in Rwanda, Grandpa didn't go with me. I traveled with my assistants. I was working with Childcare handing out appropriations for the quarter in each district of the Free Methodist Church in Rwanda. I was also finding new children to be sponsored and talking to parents, pastors and children. I loved it.

The country was unsettled; internal refugee camps had sprung up where people fled to be safe. Barriers were on the roads; soldiers searched our cars. On that trip, soldiers asked to ride with us from one barrier to the next. I told them they could ride with us if they left their guns, that we would not accept weapons in the car. They laid down their guns and got in!

Jim stayed in Kigali (capital of Rwanda) while I was on the Rwanda trip, working with Bishop Aaron at his office. I stayed overnight at an African pastor's house in Rwanda as I often did, but the next day I felt sick. I felt worse each day. By the time we got to Nigeria, I really did not feel well. Then we went north to Amsterdam and across the States to get to a church in Kansas where we were to speak. Grandpa got off the plane in Amsterdam – he was the first one off – and found us a room so that I could sleep. There weren't enough rooms at the airport hotel for everybody. It was first-come-first-served, and the rest had to wait in the airport.

We went to Kansas. Finally, Grandpa went to Michigan to speak, and I went to Seattle. It must have been a couple days after I arrived that your dad, Rick, and I took Margi to the hospital to have a baby . . . Philip. You.

The delivery went well. Since we went in the night and had been at the hospital a long time, Rick and I were going back to the house to take showers and change clothes. We planned to go back to the hospital afterwards. When we got to the house, the phone was ringing. It was Margi crying and saying, "Please, come! Philip is in the ICU." So we turned right around and went back to the hospital. Your heart wasn't working right – the doctor said that it was fluttering like a little bird. Rick went right into the ICU to be with you and Margi, who was allowed to hold you in there. I stayed out in the waiting room with friends from the church who were there for us other times throughout the years. We stood together in the waiting room praying; holding hands and agreeing together in prayer that God would touch you. Just like that, your heart began beating in correct rhythm while we were praying. The doctor was relieved and confused. You never had any more trouble after that at all. We all knew that God had touched you. It wasn't long until you and your mom were dismissed from the hospital and you came home to the parsonage near the church.

I had agreed with Margi that I would keep you in my room. When you woke up in the night, I took you into her room to nurse. Then I went back to get you and took you back across the hall after about 20 minutes. The third night after you were born, I told Margi, "I'm just going to let Philip stay with you tonight. I'm too sick to come back and get him." In the morning I said to Rick, "When you get through with Bible study and Sunday school, I wish you would take me to emergency. I really feel bad."

He said "If you want to go to the hospital, we won't wait for the Bible study to be over, we will take you now!" The friend who had helped pray for you took me to the hospital. Your father was youth pastor at the Bothel, Washington, Free Methodist Church when you were born.

When I got to the hospital, the emergency department doctor examined me. He then called an endocrinologist who just happened to be there on a Sunday taking care of another patient. The endocrinologist had a personal friend in the tropical disease department of the Center for Disease Control in Atlanta, Georgia. After they did all the blood tests, my liver function was high. I felt horrid. The doctor said, "You won't have to suffer anymore. I can give you medicine so that you won't have to suffer. But you are going to have a long rest." The tests sent to the tropical disease center showed that I had Hepatitis E, a disease that originated in India. I was the first recorded patient in the U.S. to have it. It had gone from India to Africa, and I had picked it up in Africa.

It is dangerous for pregnant women to get this type of hepatitis. They don't make it – they die. Also, another unusual characteristic of this kind of hepatitis is that the infected person doesn't turn yellow.

That was an awful night of my life, lying there in that bed in intensive care, wrapped up in tubes. I was devastated that I had brought this disease to Margi and you. I was sure that you would die, sure that Margi would die from hepatitis because I had given it to you. The whole time I was sick and handling you, I was careful not to touch you and not to breathe on you because I didn't know what I had. When the specialist came in the next day, I said, "I am worried about what's going to happen to our daughter and our grandchild, because I was with them so much when I was sick with this." He said, "I wouldn't worry about it. Do they have a dishwasher?"

I said, "Yes."

He said, "If they put all their dishes through the dishwasher, you won't pass it on to anyone in the family. You can't pass it on just by being with them. It will have to go through food or saliva." Was I relieved!

Hepatitis took a month of my life. Grandpa canceled meetings in Michigan, and came to stay with me. I was in the hospital for about 10 days. I was a month in bed at your house.

Your mother was caring for a little baby and had house guests, including a convalescent. It was the last thing she needed. I felt horrible that I was making extra work for her and your dad. But Grandpa bought the groceries and tried to help around the house. I slept my life away for a month. I was taking pain medication. And that's how we began our relationship. How can I ever forget? I love you, Philip and your brother Benjamin who was born later when we were in Africa! Grandchildren are special people!

    . . . . *and the child grew, and the LORD blessed him.*
Judges 13:24

Philip Kendall and me and Philip as a high school graduate

Chapter 16

Kigali Church in Rwanda

Rwanda and Burundi are very small countries. Each is the size of the state of Maryland. These countries are the most thickly populated part of Africa. That's part of the reason for the instability: there's just not enough space for all the people. These two small countries are on the east side of Congo. Each one has its own language that has evolved. All the Hutus, all the Tutsis and all the Pygmies in Burundi speak Kirundi. All Hutus, Tutsis and Pygmies in Rwanda speak Kinyarwanda. In the days we lived there, French was the official or business language in both countries. All government forms in those years were in French. It is different now for Rwanda because of English intrusion from Uganda. Mweya had the missionary children's school, the printing press and the Bible institute for training pastors. We went to Mweya to live and Grandpa was the director of the Bible institute.

There was a man studying in that school, who had come down from Rwanda to study in our Bible institute. His name was John Wesley Gakwaya. He already had some work experience, as he had been an elementary school teacher in Rwanda. He wanted to prepare to be a pastor and so came to our school. When he finished at Mweya and went back to Rwanda, the Free Methodist Church in Rwanda sent him to start a church in the capital city of Kigali. The Free Methodist Church was started in 1942 in Rwanda, by missionaries Frank and Hazel Adamson. The southwest corner of Rwanda was blanketed with Free Methodist Churches. They had done well there, but they had never reached out to the rest of Rwanda. It was a big deal to send this young pastor, John Wesley, to Kigali to start a church.

When we went on vacation that summer after the school year was over, we went through Kigali on our way to Gisenyi, a city on Lake Kivu, in Rwanda. We stopped to see John Wesley. He knew we were coming but didn't know when we would arrive. (He had already bought sugarcane for our children to eat. They remember him for that.) We found him sitting on the steps of his little room that he had rented; playing his guitar and singing with a group of children around him. He continued to do that, starting his church through children's meetings. He won the children. Then, through the children he won their parents to God and to the church.

There are many good things that happened because John Wesley went to Kigali. He became so well-known and well-loved in the capital of Kigali that when Bishop Aaron (the African Bishop of the Rwanda Free Methodist Church) moved to Kigali, he took John Wesley with him to all the government offices. This was Bishop Aaron's way to get in the door and get acquainted because they knew and loved John Wesley.

One mother, Dative, became a Christian as the result of Pastor John Wesley's initially winning her children. Dative went through the preparatory membership class, a training class. The day came for her and others to be baptized and to join the church on a Sunday morning. Dative had five children, and a husband who had a fairly good job, a regular income and a motorcycle. Having a motorcycle was unusual. Only people with well-paying jobs had motorcycles. Some would save up from selling some of their harvest and get a bicycle, but to buy a motorcycle one had to have a good job. Dative's husband went to work every day but had a problem—he loved alcohol. Dative tried and tried to get him to go to church with her and the children.

Finally, on the day that she was to join the church, he promised he would come to watch. When it was time to leave the house, he told Dative, "You go on ahead with the kids, I'll be there." All during the service she kept watching and hoping that he'd walk in the door, but he didn't show up. There was a reception afterwards, a meal at her house for her friends. It was a big celebration because she had joined the church. He never showed up; he was gone the whole day. She was extremely disappointed that she had gone through this celebration day without her husband. Turns out, he had stopped at a bar on his way to church and never left. He came home at night, still drunk. Dative was so angry with him she let him have it. She railed and railed at him because he had disappointed her. She was so fed up with him because he was drinking and wouldn't keep his promises.

We had a prayer meeting at the Free Methodist Church on Monday nights. People that weren't even church members came to the prayer meeting, which was quite large. Dative went on Monday night following the Sunday she was baptized. She told the people how disappointed she was in herself; that she couldn't control herself. She witnessed to the anger she had shown her husband. She hadn't exhibited a spirit of love, consideration and pity for this man who was bound by alcohol. She asked the people to pray for her to be delivered from this spirit in her that was not like Jesus. The people did pray for her. She was baptized with the Spirit of God that night. She became a new woman. She was able to endure with patience and kindness. Dative was not an especially educated person, but she was the one that started teaching the preparatory members in the church. God used her in a wonderful way.

Eventually her husband did become a Christian, but not before he had an accident with his motorcycle which left him an invalid. He was on his way home from work. He had drunk no alcohol. We don't know about the person who hit him, whether he was under the influence. The husband's conversion was the result of his wife's caring for him after the accident and showing him love and the way to Jesus. He got saved. Dative cared for him. He later died from complications of his injuries.

*   *   *

In 1980, we landed in the capital city of Kigali on Saturday. We had been in the U.S. for two years because, in our year of home assignment, some missionaries were expelled from Burundi, both Catholic and Protestant. We wrote to see if we were welcome back. We received no answer. Jim said, "No answer is a negative answer." Bishop Aaron invited us to work in Rwanda, so we had come to Rwanda from the U.S. to live. We thought we would live in Butare, but the church and God had other plans.

On Sunday morning, Pastor John Wesley Gakwaya brought us before the church and introduced us. He announced to the congregation that Jim was going to be the director of the high school at Kibogora. That was the first time that we had even heard about that. We thought we were going to live in Butare to start the Free Methodist Church there since it was a University town. African church leaders met and decided that Jim would be the director of the high school at Kibogora for a year while the current director went to get his master's degree in Kinshasa, Congo. I can still remember how shocked we both felt. We were stunned that they would do that and we would first hear of it before the whole congregation. No one had even asked Jim if he wanted to administer a school, but that's what we did. We were there for a whole year from 1980 to 1981.

Then it was time for Vernon and Sue DeMille to go to Canada for home assignment. They had been renting a house in Kigali for $1000 per month. Money was budgeted and raised to build a house near the Free Methodist Church in the suburb of Gikondo where John Wesley worked and lived. The money was spent but the house wasn't finished. The windows weren't in; the concrete floor wasn't in; plumbing wasn't finished. Nothing was finished. They had the walls in, but nothing was painted. So the mission decided that we would go live in that unfinished house. The $1000 per month already budgeted for rent for the DeMille's house for the next year would be used to complete that house.

I was working with Christian Children's Fund of Denmark and with the child sponsorship program of our church. I had a little space for a desk in the office where I worked and a table where the Africans who translated letters helped me. I was doing office work, but I felt excluded by the African women in the church. I did not understand what was going on.

The Africans thought it was horrible that we had to live in this particular house in those conditions. At first we had to carry our water to take a bath. Where we slept we had a big piece of Masonite board up against the window so we'd have privacy. We opened DeMilles' couch and slept there. DeMilles' barrels and boxes, in which they had put all their belongings, were all around the outside of this room. The floor was cemented and had screens on the windows. Our belongings were packed in the office—the outside office on the house.

It was a big house with a huge veranda on the back. We had a man from the U.S., Lloyd Phillips from Spring Arbor, Michigan, staying there with us in those camping conditions in another room in the guest suite of this big house. He and our worker, Ben Kayumba, worked hard on finishing this house. We wanted to have it in time so that when Bishop Van Valin came for annual conference and the children came home from Rift Valley Academy for Christmas, they would have their bedrooms and we would have some kind of normalcy. I kept wondering, "Well, what's my job going to be? What am I going to do in this new place?" I've been this way each time we moved to a new place.

One day an educated Catholic woman that I had never met before came by the house. She was a banker downtown but lived in our suburb of Gikondo. She said, "I see that you have this nice, big veranda here. This would be a wonderful place to have a women's class. Why don't you get tables and sewing machines and announce that you're going to have a sewing class here? You can have it after work hours, so that all these employed people that come home from offices in the city will just stop by for sewing class on their way home."

I didn't even ask for that! The women asked me! I was thrilled because I thought, "This is a way I'll have a Bible study for these women." The women found their own teacher for sewing, a skilled tailor. We started classes on the back porch. It reminded me of when the resurrected Jesus told the disciples to put their net on the other side of the boat, and they had so many fish they couldn't draw them in (John 21:3-10). Without much effort on my part, people came to God and to the church. It was as though people were hungry just for somebody to try to catch them. The class thrived; the porch was filled with people. We had our Bible study afterward and people became Christians.

After we had been meeting like that for a couple months, Dative and another woman, named Zabera, came to me before church on Sunday and said, "When church is finished, may we come to your house? We have something we want to talk to you about." They came and we drank tea together.

Finally, after telling me about their families and admiring the house, they said, "Our reason for coming is to apologize. When you came here, we said among ourselves, 'Nobody in Gikondo is going to come to Jesus because of a white woman. If anybody here becomes a Christian, it will be because black women told them about Jesus.' But we see that God used you anyway. We have come to invite you to our regular weekly Bible studies, and we want you to lead them." I didn't even have a clue those Bible studies were going on.

Africans take their shoes off outside the door; they do not walk inside anybody's house with their shoes on. One day I counted the shoes outside the door at the Bible study: 70 pairs of shoes. People were packed into the houses for Bible study.

The Catholic Church was up the hill, and the priest did everything he could to advise the Catholic women not to go to our Bible studies. They would start out like they were going to market and go through the village and end up wherever Bible study was held that week. We met in well-to-do peoples' homes. The Bible studies were popular among the women. It was like hungry birds waiting to be fed.

The priest would deny the sacraments if he found out the Catholic women were participating in the Free Methodist worship. This also happened in our Gitarama Church, which was between Kigali and Butare in Rwanda. The priest did not want his members to affiliate with Free Methodists and leave the Catholic Church. He even offered them free schooling if they would send their children to his school. On the day he asked the parents to come to enroll their children, they came to Pastor John Wesley wanting him to enroll the children in the Free Methodist school.

*   *   *

Many things happened in Kigali between 1980 and 1984. A big new church was built because the other church had been outgrown. Bishop Aaron moved there. His house was built right beside the missionaries' house, and John Wesley Gakwaya started an elementary school. He found good teachers.

There were people that were jealous of John Wesley's success. It was decided to send him way off in the hills to direct a high school. He was married and his wife was the principal of a private high school in the city of Kigali. It was impossible for her to leave her job to go with him. It meant hours of travel away from his wife, all because people were trying to demote him. That's when he came to the States to study at Kentucky Mountain Bible College. He currently lives with his family in Dayton, Ohio, a pastor to central Africa refugees who have emigrated to the U.S.

For months during the genocide of 1994, John Wesley didn't know if Virginia and his children were alive or dead. One night he had a dream that Virginia was alive. He got up the next day and told everybody at Kentucky Mountain Bible College that Virginia was alive. He was so happy. They asked, "How do you know? Did you get a letter from her?" and he answered, "No, God told me."

*   *   *

United Nations would not let us go back to Rwanda for 10 months after the genocide started in 1994. They let us return on a U.N. plane the first time. We were in Nigeria the night the Rwandan and Burundian presidents' plane was shot down near Kigali in Rwanda. We had regular reports in Kenya, where we were staying, of what was going on in Rwanda. Every day brought another awful and sad report of people who had been killed. When we finally got there after 10 months of killing, it was unbelievable to see the church in Kigali filled with strangers, Tutsis who had come to live there from Uganda and Congo. Buildings that had taken so much money and time to build were destroyed. People we had known, loved and worked with were dead.

This kind of killing is done so unceremoniously with no funeral; no opportunity for those who loved them to grieve together. It is opposite of the everyday customs of the Rwanda and Burundi people. The people of Rwanda and Burundi are polite, even when they are angry. You would never dream they could do anything so awful. Whole families were wiped out by people who knew them. Neighbors killed neighbors. The military would go to an area and stir up hatred, get a swarm going. Then the civilians would attack. They used machetes to kill. All of Dative's family was killed that way. If any Free Methodist participated, we do not know of it. We know that Free Methodists protected those of the other tribe and saved their lives.

The Rwandan woman doctor Mary Grace and missionary doctors who had been at Kibogora would stay in Bukavu, Congo, and in the morning cross the border and work in Kibogora hospital in Rwanda. They would then go back to Congo at night because it still was not considered safe by the UN for them to stay in Rwanda. Our first trips back were into Bukavu, Congo, where we'd meet with people we knew. The Free Methodist Church in Bukavu was jam-packed with refugees from Rwanda. They lived in the church. They came with whatever they could bring with them. It was all stacked around in the church.

I sent a letter to Virginia, John Wesley's wife, with Dr. Mary Grace. Virginia's parents lived right on the path from Bukavu up to the mission hospital. I knew that she could easily get the letter to Virginia. I wrote Virginia, "If you will get yourself and your children over to Bukavu, and get yourselves passports, I will see to it that you get to America, to John." The next time I went back to Bukavu there stood Virginia and her children, waiting.

The director of immigration for the government had fled to Bukavu from Kigali. He had taken all the passport blanks with him. He was giving passports to anybody that wanted to get out. That's how she got her first passport. I knew that the government wasn't stable and I figured there would be some way for her to get a passport. I didn't know it would be that easy. I got her and her children by plane over to Nairobi, Kenya, along with some church leaders.

Virginia had been living in Kigali. Thousands of people were fleeing the capital in this fighting. They had to walk over dead people in the streets to get out. They fled along with thousands of others. Virginia said her greatest fear was that in this mass of people she would lose her children. I think her daughter was only three years old then. She tied her onto her back with a cloth, and held her boys' hands. They walked all day—ran as much as they could—with all these thousands of people fleeing to Gitarama, which was a town between the capital Kigali and Butare, to get away from the fighting. We lived in Butare.

At night they just lay down in the ditch by the side of the road and slept. She said that was the coldest night of her life. When they got up in the morning, they planned to just keep on walking until she made it to her parents' house down in southwest Rwanda. That meant going through a rain forest—it was a long distance. When she woke up, there on the road was a pickup truck and she knew the driver. When he saw her he asked if she wanted to go to her parents' house. He put her and the kids in the back of the truck along with others and drove her the whole way.

While at her parents' home at Kamonyi, there was a lull in the fighting. The government announced that all the directors and principals of the high schools were to meet in Gisenyi on Lake Kivu. Graduating seniors were to go too, and they would have a mass graduation. So Virginia traveled to Gisenyi, which was all the way on the other side of Rwanda. The opposing forces knew that all these educated people were there. They attacked Gisenyi in the night, killing indiscriminately. Some people fled in the darkness and survived. That's what Virginia did. Many fled "next door" to Congo which is just across the border from Gisenyi.

Virginia paid $300 to get on a boat to go down the lake from Gisenyi, back to her parents' in Kamonyi, only to discover that a neighbor's dog had bitten her son. Her father had taken him to Kibogora hospital. She had no way to communicate, so she started out on foot for Kibogora mission hospital to get news of her son. On the way people asked, "Where are you going?" and she told them what had happened. They said, "Go back! You can't go there now! People are being killed in Kibogora. People are dying! You can't go there!" so she turned around and went back home. For 10 days she didn't know if her father and her son were dead or alive. The son and the father eventually did make it back safely, and her son fortunately did not contract rabies.

I remember calling Doctor Wilfred Fisher at Kentucky Mountain Bible College after we got back into Kenya with Virginia and the children. I said "Will you please go look up John Wesley Gakwaya? I have somebody that wants to talk to him." It was a wonderful reunion for him to hear his wife's voice and for him to know that his wife and children were alive. I tried and tried to find somebody that would escort her to the States, because she didn't know English.

Those children were so traumatized by what they had seen and heard that they would just sit; not talk, not play. That's how traumatized children behave. A child could stand against a wall all day and never move. I bought the children some toys. I found them a room in a Methodist guest house with a swimming pool in Nairobi. They stayed there until it was time for us to come home to America for board meetings.

Jim, as area director, attended the spring and fall board meetings of the mission board in Indianapolis. My mother paid my way to come to the U.S. with Jim. She said she didn't want me in Africa and all the rest of the family here. I was happy to have this way to see our children and my parents.

Later, after Virginia and her children had been reunited with John, she told me, "That was the right thing for us to stay there and debrief. Gradually, we came back to a normal way of living before we came to the States." If they had come straight from all that trauma into the States, it would have been too overwhelming for them.

What a wonderful reunion for John Wesley and Virginia and the children! It was like seeing someone risen from the dead because for days John didn't know if they were alive or dead.

Matthew 16:18 . . . . I will build my church; and the gates of hell shall not prevail against it.

This is written with the permission of John and Virginia Gakwaya.

1. Dative and Zabera
2. John and Virginia the day they became U.S. citizens.
3. Gakwaya children at the daughter Grace's wedding.

Chapter 17

John Nyoniyishyamba
and the Witch Doctor

Yohana is what they called him in Africa. That's the African way of saying John. He was quite crude, not well educated but a loyal Christian. He had studied at the lower level to become a pastor in the church. He loved to start new churches and go places where there was no church to tell the people there about Jesus. He loved to work in places where there was witchcraft, because he felt that they needed to know of God and of God's love.

In one area witchdoctors were coming to the Lord and being saved. It was wonderful to see the power of God. The head witchdoctor was angry that *Yohana* was taking all his disciples away. One time when *Yohana* was preaching, the head witchdoctor came into the congregation and blew smoke in *Yohana*'s face. He came right up to him in front of all the people and said, "If you don't get out of here and quit preaching in this place, I will give you one month to live."

Yohana calmly replied, "Sir, if you don't repent and come to God, I give you three days to live," and he went on preaching. The witchdoctor saw that the people in the congregation sided with *Yohana*, the pastor, and he left. That day, that same head witchdoctor developed an unquenchable thirst. This was a sign that his body was shutting down. He was so thirsty—he kept asking for drinks. He drank milk, he drank beer, he drank water; nothing would quench his thirst. By night, he was dead.

This incident was confirmation of God's judgment. *Yohana* exemplified the grace of God. He was willing to preach the gospel at great sacrifice to himself, with no thought of personal enrichment or favor. He obeyed a call to take the gospel to those who needed it most.

Corinthians 1:26, 27 Brothers, . . . not many were of noble birth. But God chose the foolish things of the world to shame the wise; God chose the weak things of the world to shame the strong.

Chapter 18

Strangler Fig

When we went to Rwanda from Burundi in 1980, Bishop Aaron was very interested in establishing the Free Methodist Church over the whole country. From 1942 to 1975 the southwest corner of Rwanda had been covered with Free Methodist churches. But the rest of the country lacked a Free Methodist presence. The church sent John Gakwaya to Kigali.

Bishop Aaron chose five young men, recent graduates from our high school at Kibogora, to study to be pastors and church leaders. They were stable Christians making good grades. His intention was that, while they were in seminary, Jim and I would mentor them. They were in the theological school at Butare when we lived there. They were our gospel team that we took wherever we went. When they finished school, they were sent out by the Rwanda conference to different prefectures/counties to start a Free Methodist Church. Some we took and helped them get a house. They would have Bible studies in their homes while they were trying to get the church started. Some of them were single;

some were married during that time we were with them. Some of them got married after they became pastors.

Mark was sent to the edge of the country bordering on Congo, up in the northwest corner of Rwanda, to a place called Ruhengeri to start a church. The people were very responsive. After Mark had found a site for a church, he found out that that place was formerly called Sodom because of the evil practices that dominated the area. But God performed miracles and saved a great many people. News reporters on national radio came to look over the place to see why this area that had been so difficult had come alive. They found it was the Word of God that had awakened people and caused them to repent and leave their wicked ways. From that time this place got a new name. They began to call it "The Place of God." It was also in the government newspaper: "The place called Sodom has become 'The Place of God.'"

But the enemy opposed the area, using drunkenness which brought with it many other problems for the people living there. Another problem was the worship of the idol Nyabingi, which was in direct opposition to the purpose of the church. She demanded limitless resources. There was much opposition to the gospel. Women came to worship on Sunday with wounds, their Bibles having been burned by their husbands. Their courage and faithfulness eventually led to the salvation of their husbands, who asked forgiveness for what they had done.

The children likewise suffered, often being beaten at night because they had gone to church. Sometimes they hid; other times they told the pastor about it. The youth choir members came to the pastor in tears, saying that their parents had totally forbidden them to come to church. The pastor urged them to hang on. All this time Pastor Mark had also started churches in other areas of the prefecture/ county.

It was difficult for Pastor Mark to know whom to trust, but he took this to God in prayer. God gave him a solution: counseling. He would do this in the evenings and then he started a Theological Education by Extension (TEE) program. He started the class for the evangelists who were preaching in the communes/townships near their homes, but others came also to learn. He ended up with 35 students. After teaching them awhile, he started a sort of apprenticeship while learning, so he could listen to their messages and testimonies.

The tree was called "Invincible" and grew wild with big, spreading branches in the Ruhengeri area. It was enormous with a very large trunk, but it was short. The branches spread out in every direction so that it covered an area of 330 square yards or more. The tree was called a *mugumu* in Kinyarwanda, or strangler fig. It is a kind of sycamore tree found in east Africa and it is worshiped. The tree is unusual in that shoots keep coming up or roots growing down from the outside and strangling the original, thus the name. The tree looks strange. The tree does bear fruit, but birds eat the fruit; people do not. The people credited the tree with great power. They all said that tree was what enabled them to give birth, to gain property, to harvest crops, and to accomplish many other things. People were commanded periodically to give an offering so that the family might live in peace. Pastor Mark said that from what he had heard it must have been about 200 years old. The tree was always green. It had been planted in a place where water was plentiful. The people did not know who had planted the tree but simply said it was their ancestors.

Thus the idol called *Nyabingi* was given proper respect. They said that Nyabingi was a woman whom they called *Nyabyinshi*, i.e., possessor of many—who was very rich and came from the area around Ruhengeri. Whenever anyone had an illness feared to be fatal, or was threatened by evil spirits of his ancestors, it was said to be caused by the spirit of Nyabingi. They had to pay much to propitiate her so she would leave. The tree was considered her palace. People went there to call on her for help. Many cows and goats, as well as beer, and many foods perished there. According to witnesses many celebrations and shameful practices took place there. People were turned into paupers because they had to pay so much. They even sold their gardens to satisfy Nyabingi. When the Gospel came, some decided never to return to Nyabingi. This made their families reject them.

A revival came in 1985. The people said, "Real salvation pulls out the roots. In cutting down Nyabingi, we must get rid of everything related to it. Where it has been, an avocado tree or a church must be planted for the worship of the true God."

One man, among the many that had received Jesus through the power of the Word of God, was the one who had that tree in his little garden. The garden was near the house he lived in. His wife had been blind for 10 years so all his possessions had been used for Nyabingi. All he had left was the little garden with the tree in it. He could no longer cultivate the garden because the tree had become so large that it covered the whole place. The man had become well known because so many people came there to worship Nyabingi under the tree. The man's name was Patrice Tegera, and his wife was Nyirangoragore Marie. When they were saved, they no longer went to worship Nyabingi under the tree. Many of his relatives still came to worship; they cut him off from their family because he had forsaken them and revealed many of their secrets. Tegera and his wife came to the pastor and the whole church, telling them what his family had done. The church sent people to make sure that the tree belonged to Tegera and was indeed in their garden. Then they agreed to cut the tree down to bring Tegera and his wife the relief they longed for.

Worshipers of Nyabingi believed that whoever pointed to the tree or took away a branch of it would die that same night. On May 7, 1985, 15 men went with their axes, praying that God would show that He is indeed the only God. They worked from 8 a.m. till 1 p.m. but only succeeded in cutting off two branches. They planned to return the next day. People looking on said, "Those who cut that tree are done for. They will be dead in three days."

The next day the church members said, "We want to bring it down completely." Meanwhile the followers of Nyabingi from the townships all around met to decide how they should kill the pastor who cut the tree.

That next afternoon a crowd approached, but it did not occur to Mark to be afraid. He had no idea what was about to happen. They came screaming with sticks, machetes, clubs and rocks, acting as if they were drunk or had been smoking hemp. They shouted many curses and slanders. First they ran after Tegera Patric, but he ran and escaped them. Then the crowd grabbed others of the group and pulled out their hair but they also were able to free themselves and escape. They really wanted the pastor. They said, "When the gods oppose each other, we want to see who can win." They tossed Pastor Mark in the air, ripped off his clothes, and took off his shoes, leaving only his pants in tatters. They kicked him in the stomach, on his head, and on his back. One blindfolded him. As they continued to beat on him,

Mark remembered Stephen's words, and prayed, "Lord, receive my spirit but forgive these who are doing this to me, for they do not know what they are doing." After that Mark said no more.

Those who were on top of him heard those words and said, "He's dying, and we'll be to blame." Some began to flee so it would not be counted against them. When Mark opened his eyes, he saw they had all fled, except for one who came and stepped on Mark's stomach to see if he was really dead. Then the man said, "I'll get my spear and finish him off. Maybe he is not dead."

When the man had gone, Mark felt his strength returning and felt frightened about the spear, so he got up and ran toward the city. That was not easy, because he had no shoes and was running on sharp pieces of hardened lava. Passersby thought he was crazy. A man carrying a big can of beer threw it at him. It hit him on the legs and he fell. People dragged him back under the tree and beat him again before leaving. Others came and beat him again as he lay on the ground. In the middle of all this, one who wanted to chop his neck with an axe was prevented by others. Some old women pulled him up and said, "Kill us, but leave this man of God alone." They laid themselves on top of him and refused to leave until he regained a little strength and could run back into the middle of the city. He ran with a crowd behind him until he came to some policemen who were checking a vehicle. He begged them to help him, but they beat him with their clubs, thinking he was crazy.

Not knowing where to run, he ran to the backyard of a merchant he knew, but the merchant did not recognize him. He kept shouting, "Save me! Protect me! These people want to kill me!" Then the merchant recognized him and put him in his car.

The crowd would not let the car pass, shouting, "Give us that man so we can kill him, and we'll face a trial over his body."

The merchant replied, "I'm not giving you anyone. If you don't get out of here, the one I hit will be answerable to the insurance company." He gunned the car nearly hitting people but they escaped him. He did not stop until he reached the police station. The report had already arrived at the police station. The prosecutor had already sent a car to examine the situation. Then five police returned with Mark to the tree. They began to seize people to lock up. At that point, the three-year trial began.

Friends came to visit Mark. Doctors examined him and found no broken bones. The wounds healed quickly. During the following days, people expected Mark and those with him to die but then they saw that what they always believed about the tree was not true. Mark asked that those in prison be released. Then people started to say that everyone who had beaten the man of God would die. Some did. Some came secretly at night saying, "We beg your forgiveness, because we know that everyone who struck you will die. Forgive us and ask your God to forgive us." At that time there came a strong hail storm around the tree. It pulled up the crops and killed the goats out on the hillsides. Mark begged God to stop the troubles so that the people would not be able to say that the troubles happened because the tree that protected them had been cut down.

The people took the case to court. Some of the judges came from the pagan families. When the trial began, it was not easy. The people tried to get Tegera to say that Mark initiated cutting the tree. Tegera and his wife stood firm, even though their enemies threatened them and came to kill them. The witness of those who were saved grew even stronger. The testimonies of Tegera and his wife spread everywhere. People were given unusual strength to stand up for the right.

At the time the trial began, the tree had not been completely cut down. About half of it still remained. There was nothing left to do but pray that God would destroy the tree through His own power. Mark was flying in a plane with a man of God from Scripture Union of Rwanda. Scripture Union is an organization founded in England which promotes daily prayer and Bible study. It has been very effective among the youth in African schools in winning them to Jesus and teaching them how to follow Him. It has been influential in continuing the revival in the early days of Christian missions. The man of God from Scripture Union prayed, asking God to perform a miracle. He said, "God, I ask you to send a strong wind or lightning to destroy that remaining part of the tree." God heard the prayers of His people. He sent a strong wind that pulled up that tree. When the people got up in the morning, they found the tree lying on the ground. People feared God and worshiped Him even more.

Mark asked God for 100 converts in one year. God multiplied that six times. When Mark left Ruhengeri on August 11, 1991, there were 2607 church members. The beautiful church was built.

The genocide had already begun. Some shells fell near the church. Many Christians were killed at that time. As Mark persevered with much sorrow, he had faith that they had died like the prophets of old. Mark went off to France to study, confident that he would meet those Christians again someday.

Mark's advice to those wanting to start new churches is first of all, to overcome their fear and, above all, the greatest secret is prayer.

This record was written first by Mark Rugamba for Bishop Aaron Ruhumuriza's book **A VISION OF EVANGELISM AND CHURCH GROWTH IN AN AFRICAN CONTEXT** *in 2001 and part of the record is used here by permission of the Rev. Mark Rugamba himself. I am very grateful for Pastor Mark's permission.*

Chapter 19

Mary Wambui

In 1996, we went to the Nairobi Evangelical Graduate School of Theology (NEGST) in Kenya to live and work. NEGST sits on 50 acres of land, three miles north of Karen Blixen's farm made famous by the film *Out of Africa*. When Karen Blixen went bankrupt, her 5000 acre farm was divided into fifty-acre plots along with land surrounding it for British settlers to buy. Every morning when I went out the front door of our house to walk down the hill to my office at school, I looked at the Ngong hills talked about in her book and shown in the movie.

In 1983 the Association of Evangelicals for Africa and Madagascar bought a chicken farm of fifty acres complete with the chicken coops. The settlers were not too happy about this acquisition. For the first years of the theological school, the chicken coops were used for dormitories, library, classrooms and offices. My first years there my office was in a chicken coop. Gradually, as German evangelicals and others contributed, classrooms, offices, a beautiful library, a chapel and two-story buildings for student apartments were built. As often as possible, students were required to bring their whole family to school with them. It took intensive training to earn a Master's degree. If the spouse was not qualified to study for a Master's degree, a program and curriculum were set up to educate the spouse. I followed a Mrs. Langa'at as the director of what was named the Christian Ministries Programme to teach those spouses. I had qualified teachers to help me. Those years at NEGST I called "the frosting on the cake." I loved those last eight years in Africa at NEGST!

There was a lady on campus whose name was Hannah. Everyone called her Mama Hannah. She was reliable and honest. She was the one who brought the mail from the post office each day. She cleaned public spaces and offices. Soon after we arrived on campus, Mama Hannah came directly to us and asked us to hire her daughter to help us in the house. Her daughter's name was Mary Wambui. Mary had graduated from high school, but she had made poor grades. I hired her to help. Mary would hang our laundry outside, mop the floors and wash the windows, jobs that were time-consuming for me.

Mary was a conscientious and quiet girl. She was careful and tried to do everything exactly as I told her. I said to Mary one day, "I don't think you should spend your life mopping floors and washing windows. You could do much better, much more with your life than this. I think God wants to use you some way." She applied to study in the Christian Ministries Programme that I was directing. Some of them, like Mary, had finished high school. Some had finished primary school. A couple of wives didn't even know how to read. To the ones who had finished high school, we gave more difficult studies. We accepted everybody regardless of their level and tried to build them up to a higher level. The school administration accepted Mary as a student in this program. She did well. She continued to work for me part time and went to school. She finished the program at the top of her class.

She applied to go to Pan-Africa Christian College (PACC) because she wanted to continue studying. Three girls made good grades that year. They all applied to go to PACC. The registrar at PACC said to me, "I know you; you're just a sweet old white woman that loves the girls, loves the women here. You want to help them and you just gave them good grades to make them feel good about themselves."

I answered him, "Look, I'll come back to you at the end of the girls' first semester and you say the same thing to me then."

At the end of the first semester I did see him; I did talk to him. He said, "Anybody you recommend from now on we'll accept at our school. Those girls are at the top of the class in our college." Mary finished with a bachelor's degree from PACC, and then came back to NEGST and earned her Master's degree. Now she's working in translation—a devout, dependable Christian.

Last year I had an email from Mary. This is what she said, "I got married on August 2, 2008. I also graduated from NEGST with an MA in Translation Studies in 2009. We are now members of the Wycliffe Bible Translators, and are working with the Summer Institute of Linguistics (SIL), the Sudan Branch in Juba since September 2010. I am training to be a translation consultant and the training will take five years."

I feel that God gave her the opportunity to study to become what, all along, He had in mind for Mary to do.

. . . *Lay hold of my words with all your heart; keep my commands and you will live. Get wisdom, get understanding;*

do not forget my words or swerve from them. Do not forsake wisdom, and she will protect you; love her, and she will watch over you. Wisdom is supreme; therefore get wisdom. Though it cost all you have, get understanding. Proverbs 4:4-8

Mary Wambui

Chapter 20

Elizabeth and Stephen

Elizabeth was secretary to the director of the library at Nairobi Evangelical Graduate School of Theology (NEGST). We lived on the campus as Elizabeth and her husband Stephen's neighbors from 1995 to 2004. While we were there, Stephen was put in prison. He had been the head of a bank in Nakuru in Kenya. He and all the tellers were put in prison because, one day, thieves broke in and stole the money in the bank. They were all put in prison. The director and the tellers were accused of setting up the burglary and receiving the money. In reality it was well-known robbers in conjunction with police that stole the money, Stephen has informed me.

Below is Stephen's account of his incarceration. Stephen's mother tongue is Luo, the same as President Obama's Kenyan relatives. I know Stephen also speaks Swahili and English. If you find an idiosyncrasy in his English spelling, syntax or grammar, rest assured his Luo is far better than yours.

Going to prison was an unforeseen situation that first of all gave me the greatest shock in my life. Added to the fact that I was tortured before being accused falsely, my entry into prison was the beginning of what would be a tough life for me for the next 3 ½ years. The prisons are overcrowded, even those holding remand prisoners. Mine was equally crowded.

During the first year, I stayed in a big hall (called wards) that carried over 50 people instead of the intended 15. Every space that existed was occupied somehow, including the toilets, which was just a squatting space with a small bowl for doing the call of nature. People would sleep on their sides and would turn in a "Mexican wave" at the bang on the wall by the person closest. If one missed the rhythm, they had to spend the rest of the time standing, mostly in the toilet.

Later I slept in a cell that contained 7 people instead of the intended 3. It had no toilet facilities and all had to use a can in case the need arose in the night. There was no running water and the only way to get water was to bribe the warders who would send for it. A 5 litre (about six quarts) can would go for 20/= (about 33 cents). There were lights at the wide corridors that separated the cells. Inside the cells the lighting would come from a bulb set at the corridors targeted at the cells. The plumbing that existed had long rotted.

The warders were very harsh to the prisoners and often looked for excuses to punish the prisoners. The punishment often took the form of violent physical beating using a button (baton). The prisoners would also be denied food at the whim of the warders. Those who had money, however had their way as the warders accepted bribes even of as little as 5/= (about 8 cents). There were no radios or tv then, provided by the authorities. And none was allowed in even if one could afford. Literature was restricted to Bibles and some other Godly materials after vetting.

The food was supposed to be a mug of porridge in the morning at 6 am, ugali (dough made from cornmeal, a Kenyan diet staple) and kales at lunch and ugali and beans in the evening. This was the routine everyday throughout the weeks, months and years. However because of corruption whereby the warders sold the foods, one could easily miss, their share having been sold.

Visits were allowed, however, one would talk to the visitor through a small hole that would not show the face. Contact with the visitor was not allowed, not even handshakes. One visitor was allowed per month and for two minutes. When there were many visitors, everyone would be put into a corridor and would talk to their visitor though a wire mesh. Everyone would be shouting to be heard. Even this lasted only two minutes. If one had money, they could bribe the warders to allow them to talk for as long as they wanted.

Stephen was in prison for three and a half years in Nakuru. When he had been in the prison for three years, the International Justice Mission (IJM) from the US came out to Kenya with Ryan Cobb, a missionary's son from Rwanda. International Justice Mission contacted me to ask if I had any projects in Kenya that I would like for them to work on. I gave them five projects, but in two of them the people involved had lied to me. The IJM people did not pursue cases when there were lies involved.

I told them about Stephen sitting in prison and they went right to work on it. They found out that he had, in fact, sat in prison all that time. He had never had a trial; never had his case brought up to be considered. He was just waiting in prison.

Afterwards, Stephen told me that his first year in prison he cried and grieved all the time. He was brokenhearted. It was hard for him to understand why God would let something like this happen. In his second year in prison, he became very bitter. But God worked in him in a wonderful way. His third year in prison, he started having Bible studies. By the time he left the prison, 22 men were in his Bible study. He left 22 Christians in the prison.

IJM kept going to authorities including lawyers and judge in Nakuru to find out why Stephen was in prison and his case had never come to trial. They stayed with his case and he was finally brought to trial. It was proven that he was not guilty. He was so grateful when he got out of prison that he and his wife who had been Baptists transferred their membership to the Free Methodist Church because of what we had done for him.

Stephen's time in prison was difficult for Elizabeth. She was a secretary in Nairobi and her husband was in prison in Nakuru about 100 miles away. When she first heard that he was in prison, she was devastated. She tried and tried to find out what prison he was in. When she did find out, she would go on weekends to visit him. It was a dark time for Elizabeth. When he finally got out of prison, it was a time of rejoicing. We really had a party!

Then it was time for us to come home to America. The school knew that we were going to leave in 2004. When Elizabeth first heard that we were going to retire and come home, she said, "Now, I want to know which night will be

179

your last in Africa. I want you to spend your last evening in Africa with my husband and our son and me." She said, "Now this isn't just come and say goodbye. I want you to come at 4 o'clock in the afternoon, and I want you to stay until 10 o'clock." They prepared the biggest feast I have ever had in my whole life. Other friends of ours were also invited for that five-course meal. After every course was a time of gift-giving. They gave us gifts to bring home to America. I'll never forget it. We felt very loved. That was their way of showing appreciation for what we did.

Thank God the IJM were Christians and worked hard to get him out of prison. After he was released from prison, Stephen went to Daystar University and got his bachelor's degree in Christian Ministry and Sustainable Development. He now works for IJM in Africa. He also is very loyal and active in the Free Methodist Church. People say that he's the backbone of the local church. That's how they view him. Their son Donald is to graduate in 2012 from Daystar University. At annual conference in 2012 Stephen was appointed senior pastor at the Karen Free Methodist Church that we helped start while we were at NEGST!

When you pass through the waters, I will be with you; and through the rivers, they shall not sweep over you: when you walk through the fire, you will not be burned; the flames will not set you ablaze. Isaiah 43:2

Stephen and Elizabeth

Chapter 21

Kamal

Kamal was an Iranian. He came from Southern Iran and was a member of the Bolochi tribe. His family came, when Britain controlled Kenya, to work in east and central Africa; probably his grandfather came first. Their family had built up a big business with lots of big trucks hauling supplies from the east coast of Africa into Congo and the family lived in Congo. His family was Muslim. For years there has been a struggle between Islam and Christianity in central Africa. Islam even offered free education or scholarships for university education to young people. In some countries in Africa the Muslim call to prayer over a loudspeaker is what awakens the villagers. Meanwhile, in many Congo villages, the clanging of a piece of metal against an old truck wheel rim hanging from a tree would awaken people and call them to pray in Free Methodist Churches.

Kamal's people were wealthy. Kamal heard about Jesus in Kenya, was discipled, went to church, and became a Christian. He said that the first thing that came to his mind after he became a Christian was that he had to be honest. The first thing he had to do to be honest was to stop bribing at the borders between countries to get supplies through into Congo from the coast. It was the Holy Spirit that convicted Kamal. Some call these bribes "under the table" transactions, as, in an underhanded away, you try to hand money to the person at the window for him/her to keep personally, which is less than you would pay legally. No record is kept in the customs office of a truck having passed through. Kamal's brothers were unhappy about his newfound honesty because they lost money having to pay customs. They put him out of the family when he became a Christian. His wife divorced him—she got the house and the car, and he lost everything he had. When he found a proper place to live, all his children came to live with him.

An acre of land across the road from Nairobi Evangelical Graduate School of Theology was purchased to build a Free Methodist Church. In earlier years, the government had purchased land for a paved road between NEGST and that acre where we built our church. The government had bought the land from a family, but the matriarch of the family never received the money for it. She was angry.

When we built that church, which we thought would be visible from the paved road, she built shacks along the road. Zoning ordinances required the Free Methodist Church to fence the property. She built shacks with metal roofing between the fence and the road and rented cheap rooms to people. Kamal started living in one of those rooms. He would borrow money from a Christian organization and buy things such as tomato paste and margarine and sell them to people as they passed by. At the end of the day, he would refund the Christian organization the money he had borrowed, living on the meager profits

Kamal attended our church faithfully and was in love with Jesus. There was famine in the land and he helped us with the proper distribution of relief food. We gave him a little money so he would have extra profit. He was able to rent a bigger building and have a store. He found a lovely African Christian woman and married her. A long time before that, he had asked her to marry him and she had said, "I will never marry anybody who's not a Christian." After he became a Christian, they met again. He was single and they got married.

Now, Kamal has vehicles and transports people to the game parks for a fee. He has people working for him and he also runs a guest house at NEGST where we lived.

One day, while we were still there, one of his brothers came to him with a new truck and a large sum of money. The brother asked Kamal if he would come back to the family and work with them. Kamal said, "Oh, no, I can never forsake my Jesus." Working with the family would mean going back to the old dishonest ways and Islam.

We used to have great times with Kamal when Jim was home and I got home from school in the late afternoon. School was just down the lane for me. Our homes, student apartments, chapel, classrooms, and offices were all on the same 50 acres of campus. We would have a cup of tea while we talked about what was going on in our lives and prayed together. He was one of our best friends. While he was trying to get established in the Christian way, Jim discipled and mentored him. African Christians came to Jim and told him to leave Kamal alone. They said "You're going to end up with a knife in your back. He cannot be trusted." They said that just because of his nationality. People who lack knowledge or acquaintance with anybody different from themselves learn to fear each other. A stereotype of a nationality causes people to think that everybody of that nationality is corrupt. Jim said, "This is something I have to do," and he set out to be friends with Kamal.

Kamal and his family made our lives so much richer. We had Christmas dinner together; it was special. They'd have us to their house. Even before he got married he'd invite us to his apartment that he was renting.

Kamal was winning other people to Jesus wherever he was. He still wins people to Jesus. Kamal spent time in prayer. Because he had a store, he would meet people and took every occasion to witness for Jesus. He followed the Navigator's course of Bible memorization and was friends of the people that worked in that office.

. . . . *Follow me, and I will make you fishers of men.* *Matthew 4:19*

Kamal's baptism

Chapter 22

Cars

Many places missionaries do not need a car, but ministry would really be limited without one in central Africa. The Hillsdale, Michigan, Free Methodist Church provided us a VW van when we first went to Burundi in 1965. Ours was green. The one for Kibuye Hospital that was provided at the same time was blue. Ours was nicknamed the Leaping Lizard and the other was the Blue Whale. Leaping Lizard's first trip was on a Sunday morning to take teachers for questioning to the government office in town. They were questioned to see if they were politicking. Teachers were killed in other areas, simply because they were Hutu. Jim went with them right into the office. They were released. Afterwards, they felt the reason they had been released was because Jim stayed with them.

Our third term in Burundi I had a little old Volkswagen "bug" that the children loved as much as I did. Jim bought it from a Catholic priest with some insurance money we received. It was so old that it did not even have a gas gauge. If we wanted to know how much gas was in the tank, we measured it with a stick! It carried me safely to women's meetings north and south of the city of Bujumbura. It took me up-country to Mweya to bring the children home for weekends. They have memories of the rides. We sold it when we came home to the States in 1978, to the pastor who is now Bishop Elie Buconyori. I felt like I had sold a friend. As it turned out, we were home in Spring Arbor, Michigan, for two years because of the expulsion of missionaries from Burundi. When we returned, we moved to Rwanda.

In Rwanda I had first a white VW "bug", then a yellow one, and finally a red one that let me down in the rain forest. Fortunately, a kind African friend from Kibogora came along and towed me home to Butare using a yellow nylon rope. It was all we had. The fuel pump went out. It was an old car. Dr. Doane Bonney, our mission director, happened to be there with Jim. He wanted me to fix it up, but Jim promised me the 1990 Suzuki that a retired Danish missionary had put up for sale. It was reliable and would go over any roads.

When we found out we were to be transferred to Rwanda in 1980, we were in the States on home assignment living in Spring Arbor, Michigan. Jim was traveling, visiting churches. I was working in the conference superintendent's office at the Spring Arbor Church. We were told that anything that was not personal property, like a car or a washing machine would stay in Burundi. I started looking everywhere—newspapers and used car lots and even at the mall. I was always putting our name in for giveaways. I prayed every day that God would give us a vehicle to use in Rwanda. I was very content to drive a used vehicle. I just knew that we could not do the work that the Rwanda church wanted us to do if we did not have wheels.

One day, while I was in the office, a man came in—a saint, whom we respected very much. He had visited us and worked with us in Burundi. His name was Charles Kingsley. He was the head of the men's movement in the Free Methodist denomination and a very zealous Christian. He had unique ways to build relationships with people so he could win them to Jesus. We loved to be around him and his wife. He came into the office where I was working one morning, and he said, "What do you need to go to Rwanda?"

I said, "Well, we're looking and praying for a used vehicle."

He said, "My wife and I have sold a house, and we want to help with whatever you need to go to Rwanda." When I said we needed a car, he said, "Let me go home, talk it over with my wife, and then I'll come back and talk to you." The next day he came back and said, "My wife and I do not want you to have a used vehicle in Rwanda. We want you to have the best that money can buy." So he said, "Whatever it is you want, go get it!"

Because Volkswagen parts were so easy to get in Rwanda and Burundi, and there was a big garage where VW's could be serviced, Jim liked to get Volkswagens. When we went to Kenya, he got Subarus, but that's another story. Charles Kingsley put us in contact with a man in the Free Methodist Church in New York who sold Volkswagens. Jim was supposed to go to New York for meetings. He flew there; then he took a bus on his way home to the Volkswagen place to get his new Volkswagen. He crossed the four lane highway, walking with his suitcase and his movie projector and all his belongings—he felt like a bum. However, that was the only way he knew to get across the big, active highway to the Volkswagen dealership from the bus stop. Jim went in the dealership and got the Volkswagen van. It was a conversion van. It had a big, pop-up top so that there was a double bed on top and a double bed below. It had a refrigerator and a stove, and when you folded the beds up and put the top down to ride in it, you had a nice, big space in the middle. That made it easy to pack.

Now, a side story . . . . Mike Long is now a missionary in Greece, but his father lived in Winona Lake, Indiana, He heard about our vehicle and knew that we were going to be living in this van a lot. He said "I sell bathtubs for luxury vehicles. Wouldn't you like to have a bathtub?" We always go by the maxim: "Receive whatever people give you and say thank you." Thus a small bathtub for a luxury vehicle was installed in our new van. Jim built the tub into the car so that two fisherman's seats were attached to the top of the box it was in.

Charles Kingsley bought the van and paid for its shipment to Rwanda. We put it in a big container along with the rest of our freight. A container looks like a big truck box, which can be hoisted aboard a ship. It can also be placed on a truck or train car to be moved, if necessary. Tim and Connie Kratzer put their belongings in the same container with ours to be sent to Rwanda. Tim and Connie were Free Methodist missionaries who worked at Kibogora Hospital in Rwanda and Nundu Hospital in Congo. Tim is a doctor.

When we arrived in Rwanda we had to pay an import fee, or tariff, on the van. If the van were at least six months old, we could pay the tariff for a used van. The tariff for a used van was several thousand dollars less than the tariff for a new van. When Jim went to the government office to pay the tariff, they kept threatening to charge the tariff for a new vehicle. We had owned it for six months before leaving the States and expected to pay the fee for a used vehicle. We did not have the money to pay the tariff for a new van. The officials also required the tariff to be paid within a certain time after arrival, and the time limit was really getting close. Charles Kingsley didn't have any more money; we didn't have any more money, so we prayed. One day, Jim said, "I feel I should go in and check on that car today." He went in and they had changed the rules. We got the van custom-free. That was another answer to prayer for that vehicle.

The bathtub in the van saved our lives when we moved into the half-finished house in Kigali because we had no way to take a bath in the house. Every night for weeks I would thank God for Mr. Long in Winona Lake, Indiana, who gave us that little bathtub, because it's very hot and dusty in Kigali.

When we arrived in Kigali, we brought water in with buckets until the water lines were connected. There was a hole in the wall that let the water go out in the yard. By Christmas time, when the kids came home for break, we had the plumbing installed in the house. For the three months the van was a godsend; I'm thankful for that.

That whole first term in Rwanda we drove that van where there wasn't a sign of a church to plant new churches. We always took an African pastor with us as well. We also put a little tent out over the side of the van to finish our suite. It was very, very handy. There would be vacation times and weekends that we would use the van. It was so nice to have a little stove so that any time I wanted a cup of coffee or a cup of tea I could have it, even in the middle of nowhere. That was what I liked the most.

When it became time to come back to the states at the end of that term a rich African in Gisenyi (a town in northern Rwanda on the border with Congo) contacted us in Kigali to ask if he could buy that van. He had a Volkswagen like ours. His vehicle was getting old and he wanted to buy ours. Jim said, "The only way I will sell it is if I receive cash, and enough of it so that when we come back from home assignment, I can buy a new car." The man paid us cash, just like that.

We put the money in the mission account. When it was time for us to go back to Rwanda after home assignment, the mission superintendent ordered the next car from the Catholic Cooperative in Kigali, the capital of Rwanda. For some reason the date the priest had for our picking up the car was earlier than our arrival. When we were "late" for picking it up, he decided to rent it out. It was broadsided in an accident while rented. But it was there waiting for us when we got there. Jim always wondered why one panel was not as shiny as the others and found out years later that the reason was the accident. Because of the accident, the priest sold it to us for a lower price, which was exactly the amount of money we had.

The new vehicle was a passenger van so that we could take groups. By that time, we were taking gospel teams with us. We had pastors in every province with whom we could stay, and we didn't need a conversion van as much. That is how God supplied our need for vehicles in Rwanda. The first one was blue and the next one was white, which we were still using in 1994 when the conflict began. The clutch had gone out on Jim's last trip home from Kigali. He drove it into the yard and said, "I'm not going to fool with this now, we'll work on it when we get back." There it sat until somebody fleeing from the genocide drove it clear to Congo from our house in Butare. I don't know how they got the clutch fixed, but they stole it.

They also stole my little 1990 Suzuki, my Suzuki that I loved very much. The Suzuki would go everywhere. It would climb hills and go through mud holes. It never let me down one single time in all the trips for International

Childcare Ministries I made in Rwanda. Somebody stole it, and it made me sad. When we lived in Kenya, we went to visit the refugees in Congo because we couldn't get back to Rwanda for 10 months during the double genocide. The streets of Bukavu, Congo, were packed with people fleeing Rwanda to get away from the fighting. They were all carrying their belongings. If you ever drove a car down the street you had to just crawl, because you didn't want to hit anybody. I was riding behind the driver as we went to the airport to go back to Kenya after our time there. I took out my camera and just kept snapping pictures as we drove along. When I got back to Nairobi and got the film developed, there, right in the middle of a picture, sat my little 1990 white Suzuki. There was a little brown table in front of it with Tupperware sitting on it. Right away I sent the picture to Bishop Bya'ene, the Congo Bishop, and I said, "Do something about getting my car back." That day, the Congo government took all the refugees' cars and put Congo license plates on them. My car was gone forever. When we went back later we saw it wrecked and broken down sitting alongside the road in Bukavu.

Getting a car in Kenya for our 10 years there was another story. Jim went looking for a used car. A car salesman said, "If you love your wife, you'll buy this one." I still have never figured out what I had to do with it, but anyway Jim bought it and it served us well until one night Jim was on his way home from a trip to Uganda. The Kenya conference superintendent was with him. They were stopped by the policemen who asked them if they had been in an accident. Jim and Gerald, the superintendent, could not figure out why they were asked that. They continued on their way. Suddenly they rammed into the back of a truck which had no lights and was belching black smoke so that the truck was not visible. The truck kept on going to the top of the hill where the driver stopped. Gerald asked the driver why he didn't stop when he was hit. The driver of the truck said he was afraid he would be beaten, because our vehicle was the third one to hit him. A policeman was in the truck with the driver! Jim was able to continue driving with the hood mashed in and the frame bent. I heard him come roaring in at our house and wondered what on earth had happened. The car had a choke. The frame had pushed up against the dashboard keeping the choke pulled out. We got the car fixed, but it was never the same as before. We were happy to sell it. We shared other missionary cars till we came home to the U.S. in 2000. When we went back, Jim had a Subaru Legacy and I had a Toyota Starlet till we came home for good. The Starlet became the car for missionaries to drive while in Nairobi.

You realize it is a big transition for an American to drive a car in Kenya and Tanzania. They drive on the left side of the road like people in England do. Try going on a roundabout on the left side of the road when you are accustomed to driving on the right. We would keep saying, "I had a good job, but I LEFT," or Jim would say, "I had a good wife, but she LEFT!" Left, left, left!

Chapter 23

Changes

Life in Africa was very different when we arrived in March of 1965 from what it was the summer of 2004 when we left. It was a big adjustment, even from Ohio farm life, to 1965 African technology or rather, lack of technology.

A family in Michigan had given us a wood cook-stove to take. It had a reservoir on the side where you could heat water and it had a warming oven on the top where you could keep your food warm or your plates warm. There were no microwaves in 1965 and if we had electricity we only had it from 6 to 9 at night. Our power source was a diesel generator outside the house. When we operated the generator, it was from 6 p.m. to 9 p.m. We really only used electricity to read by at night, or to be able to see to get around the house. We used it as long as we had fuel. We bought diesel fuel in barrels and hauled them in the Volkswagen van. Anyway, we took a wood cook-stove, which is what we used to cook with. However, we were living comfortably compared to the ranges some other people had.

Also, we had to buy 100-pound sacks of flour and sugar at a time. It was very hard for me to lay out that much money at once. We had to make sure we had a good place to keep it so that it didn't get stolen, didn't get bugs in it, or become damp and smelly.

Every house in Burundi and Rwanda had a storeroom off the kitchen. In ours we had metal barrels that we had shipped our belongings in from the U.S. We used these for our flour, sugar, coffee, and wheat that we roasted and ground for cereal. The storeroom also had shelves for smaller things. We had to consider all these arrangements in order to have food. We didn't go to town all that often to replenish supplies. In those days we drank more soda than we drink now. We bought a case of 48 bottles at a time, or two cases of 48 bottles at a time, and they'd last six weeks to two months. We portioned them out and they'd just be for special occasions.

We took an apartment-size propane gas range, but we'd only use it to heat water for tea or coffee when we wanted it in a hurry during the day. We would never cook anything for a long time on the gas stove. We would buy a bottle of gas and replenish it when we needed it. Gas was very expensive and often unavailable.

We had to boil all our drinking water in those days for 20 minutes. Milk would come to the door, brought by an African, and we pasteurized it by cooking it on the stove. We had a little glass weight we put in the bottom of the pan. I guess that glass weight's purpose was to keep the milk from boiling over—I didn't understand. We had to heat milk on low heat to pasteurize it. Sometimes the seller would add water to make more milk, and sometimes the water wouldn't be good-tasting water and you'd have evil-tasting milk. Sometimes the cows ate the wrong weed and produced evil-tasting milk. So milk was not my favorite thing to drink. I just used it for cooking but I would put chocolate in it so that the kids could drink milk.

We were always teaching the nationals about the importance of drinking clean water. Many people got their water where they washed their clothes and where the cows went to drink. Intestinal parasites were the big problem for the Africans and for us. Sometimes we got them too in spite of being careful. Malaria was probably the biggest problem. Nets treated with insecticide became common to prevent malaria for everyone. The Africans would get "cures" at a dispensary, just like we did.

We would buy hunks of meat from the market—hunks of beef. The bones were sold separately from the meat. In those days we couldn't get beef in Rwanda because the cattle had been killed in the conflict between the Hutu and the Tutsis in Rwanda. The Tutsi were the ones with the cattle and they either fled with their cattle or their cattle had been killed. This meant the missionaries to Rwanda only ate pork and chicken and fish out of Lake Kivu. We could get beef in Burundi, and we would just get hunks of it and prepare it. We would cut it up and can it or freeze it. We saved big pieces for special occasions for a roast. We used small pieces for stew or beef and noodle dishes. We would grind some to use like hamburger for pizza and to grill. Africans would bring live chickens to the door. We would dicker with them; buy the chickens and have to butcher them ourselves. Some missionaries had never butchered a chicken in their lives, and they found it difficult. But I had butchered lots of chickens and that part was not a problem to me. I had butchered them on the farm and I had butchered them at Kentucky Mountain Bible Institute.

I never had an electric washing machine until we went to Rwanda. From 1965 to 1980, we used a washing machine with a gasoline motor—it was loud. However, it served us well. Our refrigerator used kerosene. We had a big kerosene tank under the fridge and had to keep the wick just right. The flame had to be blue and not yellow. A yellow flame wouldn't cool right and the freezer wouldn't keep groceries frozen. It took a master to keep the refrigerator running. Jim, with his patience, always kept our refrigerator running well for us. We had a kerosene refrigerator, a gasoline-powered washing machine, and Aladdin lamps. Aladdin lamps give off a lot of heat. Aladdin lamps used kerosene for fuel. They had a mantle instead of a wick which would turn black if turned too high or the kerosene was not good. At high altitude where it was cold Aladdin lamps were adequate. but, where it was hot, Aladdin lamps were not fun. They did give the best light and were quiet. We also had kerosene pressure lamps. Each lamp had a manual pump to keep pressure. After an hour or so the light would gradually die, and we had to pump them again so that the light would be bright again.

Gardening was another big adjustment. We had pineapples right from our garden. We could easily raise or buy papayas and bananas and African-raised strawberries, so we'd get strawberries. We raised our vegetables in the garden—so we always had lettuce, carrots, radishes, and green beans and other similar produce. There's a rainy season and a dry season in Burundi. And in the dry season, you couldn't raise vegetables close to the house—you could only raise them in the valley where there'd be a stream to water the vegetables. So we had a valley garden in the dry season. I learned to plant tomato seeds in March and put tomato plants out so that it was only during dry season (which is summer in the states) that you could have fresh tomatoes from your garden. In rainy season there was too much rain and then tomatoes did not do well.

Our lifestyle was different in 2004 when we left Africa. We had been living in a modern city, Nairobi, in a suburb. I had a microwave. We had first received a microwave for our 25th wedding anniversary in 1985. Our children bought it for us, but it was stolen in the genocide of 1994. When we went to Kenya in 1995, we took a little microwave from the States. We had a gas range that we cooked on all the time. We had 24-hour electricity and electric space heaters because it was cold where we lived at high altitude. We had a space heater in the living room and in our bedroom. When we awoke, we could warm up our bedroom. It would sometimes be 50 degrees Fahrenheit in our house, so you know, it was cold.

Telephones were another story. Of course we did not have them in our houses when went in 1965. We used telephones at the post office. It would take about two weeks to get a letter from the States; it often took longer. We could send telegrams, but the communication with the states was difficult, and took a long time. We posted telegrams at the post office. When we moved to Bujumbura we did have a telephone, but it was still difficult to communicate. If we could get through to the U.S., it was often difficult to hear. During political unrest around 1990, cell phones spread through Africa like wildfire. We used cell phones in Africa before people used them in the States because the landlines were not good in Africa. I remember that some cell phone company advertisement had a picture of a Masai tribesman standing there in all his regalia in the middle of nowhere, talking on a cell phone. That's really the way it was. When we visited Burundi from Kenya, it was unstable politically. When we walked off the plane, our African church leaders would give us a cell phone and they would say, "Don't go anywhere without this cell phone. If you need help, here's the number that you dial on this cell phone." They consistently had the ability to communicate with each other on cell phones. It was such a surprise to us, when we came home to the U.S. for board meetings, that people here weren't using cell phones. That's one time that the speed of modernization was faster in Africa than it was in the U.S. Texting was also done much earlier than in the U.S. When Jim was away at meetings during the ten years we lived in Kenya, I always had contact with him by cell phone wherever he was. It made it easier for me to let him go because I had a way to communicate.

In 2004, I had an answer to prayer. Remember when we went to Rwanda and I couldn't take the washing machine and car with us from Burundi? An elderly man from Bedford, Indiana (who has gone to heaven now) traveled with us on that trip. We stopped in Kenya on our way into Rwanda and he bought us a washing machine. It had an agitator on one side and a spin dryer on the other. We washed our clothes on one side and then rinsed them on the spin dryer side. The clothes would be almost dry when they came out. I used that washer the whole time that we lived in the Kigali house. When we moved to Butare, my sister Bee gave us money to buy a washer and a dryer. There was a second, little dryer that we received for no extra cost. I let it sit in the garage. When they stole our possessions in the genocide in 1994, the malcontents couldn't get into the room where the washer and dryer were. The room had no windows, and a metal door, which was locked. So they never stole the washer and dryer. It was too big and expensive to move to

Kenya so I sold it to World Relief and our friends Willard and Doris Ferguson used it.

Willard and Doris were our friends from French study days in Belgium. They were also our co-workers at Mweya in Burundi. Their home was completely demolished down to rubble during the genocide. They were living in Kigali, Rwanda, at the time. They had a church started for the Evangelical Friends in Kigali. When World Relief came to help rebuild, Fergusons worked for World Relief.

I sold the washer and dryer for about the same amount of money that we paid for them. When we got to Kenya, we bought another little washer with the spin dryer on the side and that's what we used to wash our clothes. We would hang the clothes out on the line.

One time we went back to Rwanda when we were living in Kenya, and there, on the back porch of the house we had lived in in Kigali, sat that little dryer that someone had given for free with the big dryer. The missionaries living there in Kigali were not using it—it was all covered with dust and dirty. I cleaned it and I got an African friend to give me a carton that it would go in. I put it in that carton and took it back to Kenya as luggage on the airplane. We used that until we came home to the states in 2004. I was so happy to have a dryer again.

I don't think we ever had Internet. I don't recall it even in 2004. It was at the school, but we only did e-mail. That's all anybody did. It was slow and we had to have patience to use it. I would only check email once a day after school, when Jim was gone.

We had Indian restaurants and fast food places in Nairobi, and nice restaurants, too, so it was very different from how life was when we first went. We had always been through Nairobi, coming and going, but we would stay in mission guest houses with non-Free Methodist denominations. There was a big change in Nairobi in that Kenyans moved into the city. The city could not keep up with the need for water and electricity with the increased population and sewage was a big problem. Regardless, people would keep moving in like they do everywhere.

Chapter 24

Rusumo

When we moved to Rwanda, we were working with Pastor John Gakwaya in the capital city Kigali. One of our assignments was to drive out to help the people in Rusumo. They were Free Methodists from southwestern Rwanda and were moved clear to the other side of the country right on the edge of Tanzania. The land was a rugged area rather desert-like: low, scant rain fall, hot and no nearby marketplace. With no church and no school they were literally planted out in the middle of nowhere while the government took over their former fertile land for tea plantations. The government called it expropriation but they did pay them so that they could buy land on the eastern side. We were sent to help those people build a church. Because of the huge rocks everywhere—there was no road—we had to walk maybe a couple miles to where the people lived in a place called Rusumo.

We went, first with Pastor John, to visit them. Then some ways opened up for us to get a church built and a school to help the Rusumo people. Christian Children's Fund in

Denmark offered to help us. They were already helping us in southwestern Rwanda with a school for children who were dropouts because of either poverty or they were mentally challenged. Christian Children's Fund helped us in Burundi with schools

Another way we received money to build the church and school was with the Charles Kingsley Memorial. Charles Kingsley was the one who gave us the money to buy the best car that money could buy when we moved to Rwanda. We built the church in honor of Charles Kingsley with contributions from his family.

When the Christian Children's Fund CEO was to come out to Rwanda to survey the projects, Jim said, "I can't ask a man who's used to living in the city and having modernity at his fingertips all the time to walk two miles to see where we want to build." He bought sledge hammers and a crowbar of some kind to pry the rocks out of the ground. He told the people he was giving them the tools to carve a road that would accommodate a car to get to the site of the church and school. Jim said, "I'll give you a month, we'll be back in a month, and we want to be able to drive through here." Those people worked and worked, and, when we went back in a month, they had that road carved out.

Many interesting things happened while driving back and forth on that road. One time we hit an ant hill and bent the tire rim. Once I fell into the thistles trying to help push the car out of the mud when for once we did have a rain. Anyway the road did take us to the people. The trips did make something to write home about!

We built a social center. It was both a place of worship and a school for the children. Christian Children's Fund and the contributions in honor of Charles Kingsley worked together to get the site built there. The church continued and it has thrived like Free Methodist Churches thrive in central Africa.

That he might present it to himself a glorious church, not having spot, or wrinkle, or any such thing; but that it should be holy and without blemish. Ephesians 5:27

Chapter 25

The Call From
The Rain Forest

The Chinese government, to pay back a loan they had from Germany, agreed to build a road through the rain forest in Rwanda, from the west clear across to eastern Rwanda. Germany had asked the Chinese to help Rwanda instead of paying them back money the Chinese had borrowed from Germany.

The road would be built at high altitude, where you could see exotic birds and animals in the rain forest. It was just trees at the time—nobody lived up there. Every trip we made from Kibogora to Butare was eventful while they were building that road. Butare was a university town where we were starting a Free Methodist Church when we lived at Kibogora. Sometimes the road would be closed and we'd have to go around another way. We'd always get stuck or have a long time to wait because the road was closed or something—there was always an event. One time while we traveled through, we saw a moonbow—a full moon and a rainbow in the sky in the dark. It was fantastic.

High in the mountains of Rwanda—where it is always cold and rainy—is an unlikely place to plant a church. But it rates at the top for natural beauty. You may see baboons or blue vervet monkeys as you travel or turaccos (a very shy colorful big bird). I always looked for the elephants that locals said roam in the rain forest but I never saw one. The pre-historic fern and virgin forest always made the first-time viewer gasp with awe.

However, in the most thickly populated part of Africa where people live on what they harvest, where the soil is depleted, where the farms are growing smaller as they are divided among the sons, retaining a rain forest for its natural beauty is not a priority. Year by year the farmers gradually chopped away at trees and the gorgeous forest was quickly becoming a thing of the past. Then ecologists saw that Rwanda needed those trees if she wanted to continue to receive adequate rain fall and not be part of the desert. Inquisitive researchers saw that people could be taught to raise foods that grow well at high altitude, such as wheat, white potatoes, and corn. The scientists saw that the hills could be reforested.

The European Common Market granted 14 million dollars and later 22 million dollars to set up this training, reforesting project. They named the project the Zaire-Nile Divide Project. Dr. James Gasana, who earned his doctorate at the University of Idaho in the U.S., was chosen to serve as director. After project offices and personnel homes and roads were built and extensive research by Europeans was completed, it was time for the project to begin in earnest.

1000 Rwandan families moved into the area. These were people from other parts of Rwanda whose farms were too small to support their families. These 1000 families were given tile to roof their new homes, seed to plant, and lessons in good farming methods.

The project also included an elementary school for the transplanted children to attend—a lovely school built of burned brick with a metal roof, cement floors and blackboards.

Director Gasana started asking the Free Methodists what they could do to provide a church home for these 1000 families. Bishop Aaron Ruhumuriza and Jim Kirkpatrick, the Butare district superintendent, started visiting the project on their way to and from Kibogora. They were looking for a church site, and one day they spied it. It was the perfect place, a hill with a flat top not far from the project's elementary school. This hill had not been given to anyone else for building. To our delight, we discovered that the next five year plan for the project was to let 1000 more families move in and our requested site was right between the two groups.

After Paul Nzacahayo graduated from Butare Theological School in September 1986, he was sent to be the first pastor. There was no church, no parsonage, so where could he live? After looking around, pastor and superintendent found a house about twelve miles away. Have you ever tried to walk that far? A kind Christian in the U.S. heard about Paul and provided a motorcycle so he could get back and forth to our hill. Paul also became a chaplain for the workers in the project who were busy planting trees. The people at Mushubi, where we found a house for Paul, wanted Paul to be their pastor. He started with a Bible study in his home, then a Sunday morning service. Hungry-hearted people came to the service and their lives were changed as they met Christ. Now those people have their own church building.

People living around the original church site called Paul their pastor and said, "When you get a church built, we will come." First, we found some money and built Paul a house made out of sun-dried brick. Then Paul got married to a Christian teacher who was employed in the local school.

How were we going to get that church built? The contract with the European Common Market stated that none of the money was to be spent for religious purposes. The director told us the church had to be built well in keeping with the project buildings. We prayed and wondered, "How can we get that kind of money?"

Then the time came for Eldon and Gerry Gudgeon to go back to Warm Beach, Washington, from their work in Congo. They decided to fly home out of Rwanda. They happened to stop by our house when Paul was there and heard his story. They later told us that, while they were sitting there, God told them, "You are the ones that are to help that young pastor build that church." They went home to Warm Beach, Washington and set to work raising money to build that church. They stayed with the project until it was finished. When they returned, they lived right up there at the project.

I wish you could have seen that beautiful church. The building was everything Director Gasana wanted. Just think of the opportunity: the only church for all those people. We had the privilege of presenting the claims of Christ in another area.

The people were happy and responsive to the teaching. From the very beginning they packed out the church which was a rather large building. The people came to Jesus in a wonderful way. Sometimes I ponder the extravagance of God's help in spreading the Gospel in places where there was no other church during those years that we lived in Rwanda.

Chapter 26

Coffee

In an earlier chapter I told of how Kirk and Faye passed on to us many of their household goods. One gift Kirk gave us was a big metal barrel full of sacks of coffee beans. Each sack was marked with the year he had bought it. He gave us the coffee at the same time he gave us the rest of their things. For eleven and a half years, he had bought some at harvest time from African farmers. Left over from Belgian control were the coffee and tea factories and strict rules about how to care for them. Also the farmers had laws to follow about the care of coffee trees and tea bushes.

If you haven't tasted Burundi coffee, you have not tasted the best. It is very smooth, strong, and aromatic. Burundians raise two kinds of coffee: mountain grown robusta and valley grown arabica. It was a delight to drive through the valley out of Bujumbura when the coffee trees were flowering. I can still smell the fragrance. Interestingly, you never have to watch out for insects getting into the coffee beans. Coffee beans aged at least a year are the best. We would not roast the coffee until we were ready to use it, one skillet at a time.

When that was finished, we would roast more. We roasted the beans in the oven of the wood stove in an iron skillet. Then we ground them in a hand grinder every morning with a grinder given to us by Dick and Barbara Ackerman from Pulaski. We continued using the mechanical grinder until the racial strife in 1994. Then our daughter Margi/Meg gave us an electric grinder when our treasured grinder was stolen.

We worked on that barrel of coffee for perhaps six years. Then we bought from local African farmers when Kirk's coffee was finished. My impression is that when we first went to Burundi, coffee was more of a cash crop than a drink the Burundians enjoyed. We would be served tea with lots of milk and sugar in it but hardly ever coffee. I think the people in Burundi drink more coffee now than they did 40 years ago.

Folklore has it that an Ethiopian goatherd noticed goats dancing after they ate cherry-red berries from a bush. The goatherd ate a few and then danced with the goats. It is said that he went home to tell his wife, who told him he had to tell the priest. Then a monk picked some of these berries and shared them with his brothers in the monastery. That night they were more alert in their prayers. In the National Geographic history of coffee, a record is given of the first power bars made of coffee and animal fat.

Coffee later crossed the Red Sea from Ethiopia to Arabia. Wherever Islam went, coffee went too. It is said that Arabia and Ethiopia made the coffee beans infertile by boiling or parching the beans. This prevented the coffee beans from being transported as seed to other countries and planted. No coffee bean sprouted outside Africa or Arabia until the 1600's. Tradition has it that Baba Budan left Mecca with seven fertile beans strapped to his belly. I don't know who Baba Budan was, but he became famous as the person who started the raising of coffee in other countries. This was the start of the agricultural expansion to Europe and their tropical colonies.

Ethiopia and Eritrea's coffee ceremony is an integral part of their social and cultural life. An invitation to attend a coffee ceremony is considered a mark of friendship or respect, and is an excellent example of Ethiopian hospitality. Performing the ceremony is almost obligatory in the presence of a visitor, whatever the time of day. Don't expect it to be done in a hurry though. The ceremony can take hours.

The ceremony is usually done by a young girl in a white cotton dress with colored woven borders. The roasting of the coffee beans is done in an iron skillet or pan over a tiny charcoal stove. The pungent smell mingles with the scent of incense which is always burned throughout the ceremony. When the coffee beans have turned black and shiny and the oil has come out of them, the girl walks around the room, carrying the pan, and lets everyone smell the aroma. Then the beans are ground with a mortar and pestle. The ground coffee is slowly stirred into the black clay coffee pot filled with boiling water. The coffee pot is locally known as *jebena*, which is round at the bottom and sits on a ring somewhat similar to what the central Africa women put on their heads when they want to carry a load. The coffee pot has a lid made of straw. They usually strain the coffee through a fine sieve several times. The youngest child is sent to announce the coffee is ready to be served and that she is ready to bring a cup of coffee first to the eldest in the room and then to the others, connecting all the generations. Finally the coffee is served in tiny china cups to all who are there who have waited and watched the procedure for the past half hour. Gracefully, the girl pours a thin golden stream of coffee into each little cup from a height of one foot without spilling a drop. Coffee is taken with plenty of sugar but not milk and is usually accompanied by lavish praise for its flavor and skillful preparation. Often it will be served with a snack food like popcorn or peanuts. In most parts of Ethiopia, the coffee ceremony takes place three times a day. It is the main social event within a village. If invited into a home to take part, it is impolite to leave until you have consumed at least three cups, as the third cup is considered to bestow a blessing.

We were privileged to participate in the coffee ceremony during our years in Kenya. Our next door neighbors at NEGST were Eritreans who had lived for years in Ethiopia before coming to Kenya. We participated with them, as well as with the Ethiopian students I taught. When one Ethiopian graduated, she gave me her Ethiopian coffee pot to bring to the States. I treasure it.

Coffee holds a sacred place in Ethiopia. In a world where time has become a commodity, the Ethiopian coffee ceremony takes us to a time when value was given to conversation and human relations.

Psalm 103:5 Who satisfies your mouth with good things; so that your youth is renewed like the eagle's.

Chapter 27

Beth

The year was 1976; we were in our third term. We lived in Bujumbura, the capital of Burundi, and we had four children. Beth had finished eighth grade and was doing correspondence for high school because she kept telling us that she did not have long to be with us. At that time we understood her to mean that soon she would be going to the U.S. for university and she wanted to spend her high school years with us. She did not want to go away to Rift Valley Academy in Kenya where her dad and his brothers had gone 1000 miles away from where we lived. We agreed with her and let her stay home. Margi and Ed and Len were all in boarding school at Mweya in the hills.

We lived down in the valley where it is very hot all the time. At that time, Jim's brother Tim and his wife Pat were also out there. Tim was the director of the Christian radio station in Bujumbura. In English it was CABCO (Central African Broadcasting Company).

My sister Barbara and her husband Howard Clayton were working with the Christian radio station also. They lived high up at 7200 to 7500 feet altitude on one of the highest mountains in the country, in a house built by Belgians in colonial days before they turned the government over to the Africans. The Belgians had built houses there—nice houses. There were lots of flowers. They had also built a pottery factory below in the valley. People called Nyakarago, the site of the antenna, the pottery factory, and where my sister and family lived, the Garden of Eden. There were steps down to the waterfalls and to the pottery factory that the Belgians had built. It was such a beautiful place. You would have to see it to know how pretty it was. Barbara and Howard lived there and cared for the antenna of the Christian radio station.

At the Claytons, it was cold. We wore winter clothes when we went to visit them. They always had a fire in the fireplace, especially when rainy season came in the winter. It was an isolated place in the country. At that time there was one paved road through the country, which passed the radio antenna site. However, this was a neglected part of the country. For 20 miles in any direction of the radio antenna site there was not a school, not a market, not a clinic, not a church. Very few adults there knew how to read. They had never had opportunity to learn or to go to school. Barbara and Howard, naturally, felt very concerned. They wanted to help those people.

Jim went to the governor and asked if we could build a church there. But the governor refused unless we planned to build a nice church with walls of burned brick or stone with a good roof. It could not be mud walls with a grass roof. He said, "It's beside the only paved road in the country, and we want everything along the paved road to be nice." We didn't have any money to build a "nice" church.

I should say here that an owl had decided to live in our backyard. An owl is a bad omen to an African. Our guard and house-help tried diligently to chase that owl away and even to kill him, but they could not. They were convinced that something bad was going to happen to us. And it did!

* * *

One day, we were there visiting and either Barbara or I said to the other, "I wonder what it will ever take for us to get enough money to build a church here." Two weeks after we said that to each other, Beth went with Barbara and Howard to stay with them for the weekend. They had been down in the city and they took her back with them. We lived about an hour from where Barbara and Howard lived. Their daughter, Terry, had been sick and she was home from boarding school. She was still home that weekend, so Beth went to spend the weekend with her. I was at Mweya in some board meetings, and Jim was in Gitega (the local government town) in a meeting for the cooperative Christian literature program for the country.

About 11:30 on March 20, 1976, we were out of our meeting, and I was visiting with Della Land, a Free Methodist missionary from Snohomish, Washington. She was caring for a little orphan African baby. I heard a car come to their house. I went out with the little baby in my arms and Jim was there. I said, "You sure got through your meeting early."

He said "I have something to tell you. You need to sit down some place."

All at once, when he said that, I knew something bad had happened. I felt . . . cluttered—I guess that's the only word I know to use—holding that baby. So I quickly took the baby inside and found a place to sit down outside.

Jim said, "Beth has died."

Beth and Terry had gone for a walk on Saturday morning, about 9:30. Terry had already climbed onto a rock that was about six feet high, and she was holding onto Beth trying to pull her up. Beth's shoes slipped. Terry wasn't strong enough to hold her. Beth fell back and hit the back of her head, landing beside a little stream. Terry went running and told the workers higher up somewhere that Beth had fallen. She went to her mom in the house and told her, "I think that Beth is dead," because Beth never said anything to her at all. Howard came running with the workers.

One of the houses was rented to a very good Indian friend of our families, named Jay Mandavya. There are no more hospitable friends than Indians. When he heard about the catastrophe, he had Barbara, Howard, and Terry put Beth in his car. What usually took an hour, he drove in 25 minutes. He flew down to Bujumbura to the doctor with Beth and Claytons. We had a German lady doctor as our physician. She pronounced Beth dead of a broken neck. Claytons contacted Jim's brother Tim, who worked at the radio station in Bujumbura. Then Jim's brother Tim had to call Jim in Gitega and tell him that Beth was gone.

I remember when we went to tell them, Ed and Len and Margi were eating lunch. The other two Clayton girls, Sandy and Ginny, were also there. It was decided that James Morris, Evangelical Friends missionary working at the radio station who was up-country for the committee, would drive us down to the capital. It took about three hours to get to Bujumbura from where we were at Mweya.

The children sang "Through It All" by Andrae Crouch. They sang that song in the car on the way down. When Jim came to Mweya to tell me that Beth was gone, the very first thing that came to my mind was, "Well, she's *safe* in the arms of Jesus."

It was a convincing thought, as if you were traveling around the world; going to Africa or somewhere far away, and you called back to say you had a safe trip. The person back here that loved you would be relieved to know that you had made it safely there. My feeling was much stronger than that but it was similar. Just like, "Well, this is what we've been looking forward to all our lives for all of us." I was convinced that Beth was safe. The night before she died, she had told Terry that she knew that, if anything happened to her, she would go to be with Jesus.

We got down to Bujumbura and they had Beth lying on her bed in her bedroom. Pat had asked Eleanor Johnson, a Plymouth Brethren missionary and our friend, to prepare Beth's body. They put the dress she had worn for her eighth graduation on her. Jim and Tim went right away to the Catholic cooperative and discovered there was one wooden casket left, which they bought. They brought it back to the house and family placed Beth's body in it. I do not remember seeing Beth before they laid her in the casket, but Jim does.

Willard and Doris Ferguson who lived in Kibimba at the time at the Friends hospital and secondary school came to our house. It is traditional in Burundi for someone to stay up all night with the corpse when someone dies. We called it a wake. Willard and Doris stayed up all night at the house. It was very hard for us to sleep; Jim sat up in bed and cried. I don't know if he slept at all that night. He cried and cried. I have never seen him before or since cry like that. He was so broken. I felt paralyzed, like feeling was gone, like the shock was too much.

The next morning we got ready for the funeral. It was Sunday morning. People kept coming to the house to sit with us. Gerald and Marlene Bates were among the first to come from Bukavu in Congo to cry with us. Our Beth and Margi and their David and Bill had grown up together.

We had only one place in Burundi where our mission had permission to bury white people. That was Kibuye hospital, where we had started out, on beyond Mweya. It was still another hour to get there from Mweya. We all drove up there for the funeral in a caravan. Doris and Willard Ferguson, who had stayed up all night at our house, sang the song "Safe in the Arms of Jesus" at the funeral. The missionary children sang a special. Gerald Bates and Jim Morris spoke in the service. People came from everywhere for the funeral. After the funeral, we went to bury Beth in the grave that had been dug. Grave preparation and the protocol for the funeral were all supervised by Earl Terman from Spring Arbor, Michigan, who was at Kibuye in a building program.

In Africa, all the people that come to the funeral throw dirt on the coffin after it's lowered into the grave while a committal ceremony takes place. I couldn't stand it. I felt like I would die. I couldn't handle seeing people throw dirt on that casket. I don't think any African understood me, but I told Jim "I can't stay here." A little guest house had been prepared for us to stay the night. Jim and I walked over to that house and sat down while they buried Beth.

Betty Ellen Cox, a Free Methodist missionary, who had been our Kirundi language teacher, was a translator missionary living on that station. She had moved there from Kibimba where she had been teaching in the high school. She prepared the dinner for all the people that came to the funeral. She believed it was a miracle that there was enough food for all—far more people than that which she and her helpers had prepared. The food never gave out till she was done serving. She felt that God had multiplied it. After that, the Claytons and we took our kids out of school and spent a week at Kibimba. Kibimba was between where Beth died and where the kids went to school, where Doris and Willard lived. There was an empty house there. In that time Jim and Tim crafted a letter to tell everybody in the states that Beth was gone:

Dear friends,

We want to share with you some of the events that have come to us in the past few days. On Saturday, March 20, 1976, our Beth went to be with Jesus. Martha and I were in the interior of Burundi for the weekend doing church work. Beth was at Nyakarago, the Radio CORDAC transmitter site. She had wished for some time to spend a weekend there with her Aunt Barbara and Uncle Howard Clayton. Saturday morning she went for a walk in the hills with her cousin Terry. While climbing a ravine where she had gone often, she slipped and fell. She died instantly. She was buried the next day Sunday at 3:00 P.M. at our Kibuye mission. We share with you the obituary written by her Uncle Tim (Charles) Kirkpatrick. Providentially her Grandfather Kirkpatrick got the word in time while in Rwanda and was able to be with us for the funeral.

For various reasons Beth chose not to go back to school in Kenya after Christmas, but rather to study at home. These were her happiest days. She blossomed in her studies and set herself to be friendly to all she met. Her aim in life was to be a lawyer so that she could help the underprivileged.

Beth told her Aunt Barbara that life was short and that she wanted to be with her parents while possible. Her last evening she read her favorite Scripture passage, I Corinthians 13, to her cousin Terry, and stated that if she should die she knew she would go to heaven. Later on we found this statement in her own handwriting: "It is required of loved ones to be apart for a time, and while they are absent one from another, their souls do bear company."

Some would ask why this should happen. We can only say it was the hand of the Lord. She was loaned to us for fourteen happy years. Now we have the sweet confidence from her life, from God's Word, and from the Holy Spirit that she is "safe in the arms of Jesus." In the final analysis that is our highest goal for our children.

We want to thank our many friends, some of them made during this time, for their kind help and expressions of sympathy. Many have asked about a memorial for Beth. We would like, the Lord willing, to build a chapel at Nyakarago, the place of her home-going. The people of that area have long asked for a church.

Meanwhile we want to be faithful to let people know that Christ can give them new life. The message we preach of salvation in Christ, of sanctification by the Spirit, of life after death are wonderfully demonstrated in a time like this. Praise the Lord !

In His love,
Jim and Martha and family

OBITUARY

Elizabeth Faye Kirkpatrick, known to her friends and family as "Beth," was born on October 15, 1961. A keen sensitivity to the things of God characterized her life. At the age of two she first spoke to her parents of a sense of personal guilt and was led by them to give her heart to Jesus. This awakening to spiritual reality grew and blossomed as the years went by.

A cheerful, friendly attitude and a readiness to talk to others about her Lord were evidence of the spirit that Beth's life expressed.

She went home to be with her Lord as she was engaged in one of her favorite activities, enjoying to the full the beauty of the out-of doors.

Beth Kirkpatrick's departure leaves a large, empty place in the hearts of her parents, Virgil and Martha, her sister Margi, her brothers Ed and Len, relatives—many of whom are in Christian service, and numerous friends. They sorrow, but not as those who have no hope. They enjoy the happy prospect of seeing Beth again some day, through Him who said, "I am the RESURRECTION and the LIFE!"

Remember, it was VERY difficult in 1976 to phone to America. Our Indian friend, Jay, found an adequate connection with the States for us probably by bribing the phone company. We called my mom and told her that Beth was gone. When she got the phone call she was up on a ladder papering the dining room. When she got climbed down, it was to hear that Beth was gone.

It was so hard for my mom and dad and for Jim's mom to get the news. Grandpa Kirk, Jim's dad, was out in

Rwanda, so he came down to Burundi for the funeral to be with us. The people in our church, at home, the Oak Grove Church of the Brethren, where I grew up and where Jim and I were married, decided to have a memorial service that next Sunday for Beth.

It was on our way down to where Beth's body lay in Bujumbura with our car full of our children and nieces and Jim Morris and Jim and me that the thought came to Jim and me at the same time as we passed Nyakarago where Beth had died: "We'll build a church here in memory of Beth!" It seemed strange afterwards; how we looked at each other and said this to each other, how that thought came to us both at the same time. When we got to Bujumbura and phoned to the States, we told them that was what we wanted to do. It was wonderful how people gave money to build that church.

The next weekend, after that extended stay at Kibimba, we were supposed to go to a big youth retreat in southern Burundi. I told Jim, "I can't go. I just can't face being with people yet." So he went. I stayed with Claytons at Nyakarago where Beth died. All night long I heard that little brook rippling past my window. I heard the waterfalls. I could not sleep. I never slept at all. The grief was horrible.

Soon after money started to come from the States to build the church, Jim bought a piece of land just up the hill from where Claytons lived, between them and the paved road. The governor let us start having worship services on Sunday in the old pottery factory in the valley that had been built by Belgians in colonial days. The whole countryside turned out for the church services. Everybody came. When we finished the service on the third Sunday, the village chief asked us missionaries and the African pastor to sit down. We, the Claytons, and an African pastor that the superintendent had given us to help with the worship, sat down.

The congregation made a circle in the pottery factory. It was a big room and they all stood huddled together. The chief stood up in front and said that this is what the people wanted him to tell us: "For many years, the people in this area have said 'God does not love us like He loves other people.' Other people have churches and schools and clinics and markets but we have nothing. God does not love us like He loves other people. But now that you have come, we know God loves us. So we are standing here today to tell you that we all want to follow Jesus, we all want to be Christians, and we all want to join the Free Methodist Church."

We all cried for joy when we heard the chief's speech.

The church had membership training classes every week as were held in all the churches. There were lesson plans for the pastor to follow to help the people know the Bible, the way of salvation, the core principles of the church, etc. This book was prepared long ago by Betty Ellen Cox. The first three months are devoted to salvation: the basic plan of salvation and surrender. The second three months are for membership training. Remember they had been worshiping in the pottery factory in the valley till the church was built. It was a big membership training class, as well as a big baptismal service! Free Methodists pour, sprinkle, or immerse, whichever the person to be baptized desires. It is my recollection that we sprinkled there. Some had been baptized as babies in the Catholic Church, so we respected that and did not baptize again.

It was wonderful that we had Howard Clayton, my brother-in-law, there. He helped with the building. We had an African named Mbogoye that had been taught by Burt McCready. Our children knew Burt from Spring Arbor. Burt had been a missionary, a builder. He had taught this man, Mbogoye, how to build. Mbogoye had a group of Africans to help, and they built this church of stone they had gathered from the waterfall where Beth died. Howard built a beautiful pulpit and engraved on it that he did it in memory of Beth.

The name of the church is Nyakarago Free Methodist Church. Everyone knows it is the church in memory of Beth but we chose not to put her name on the church.

In 1978, it was time for us to go home to America for home assignment. Before we went, we dedicated that church. That's when our children were baptized and joined the Free Methodist Church. There was a visitor with us, Milburn Wills, from John Wesley Church in Indianapolis. He had come out because members of another Indianapolis church, West Morris Street, had built a clinic at Kibuye hospital in memory of a Free Methodist doctor who had died. Milburn was with us for the dedication of the church.

Soon we were on the plane on the way home to the U.S. It was eight hours up to Europe from Africa; a layover, then eight hours across the Atlantic to America. Sometime while traveling I was sitting in my seat, not even thinking about Beth who had died two years earlier. All at once the verse from Genesis chapter 50 came into my head. Only this is how it came to me: "Satan meant it for evil, but God meant it for good, to save many people."

In the Genesis story Joseph had revealed himself to his brothers and they thought he would be mean to them for all that they had done to him. Instead Joseph said "You meant it for evil, but God meant it for good, to save many people" (because of that famine). All at once, I realized that Satan had tried to destroy us; tried to make us give up and quit and leave Africa. But God used Satan's actions to cause many people to know about Jesus. Building the Nyakarago church and reaching the people had to have been a miracle, for the area was so neglected.

Since 1976, when Beth died, there have been difficult times politically in Burundi. There have been wars, skirmishes and other difficulties between the tribes in Burundi. Other churches have come to that area. I should say that Christian Children's Fund of Denmark helped us build a school beside the church, a burned-brick school so that grades one through six could have an adequate building with qualified teachers. When we started that school, we had older youth going there for first grade; they were learning to read because they never had an opportunity to learn before. People were extremely grateful to be able to learn to read.

In the conflicts that happened later, other churches got destroyed in the area. Miraculously, nobody ever touched that church. The windows were never stolen. The doors were never touched. The roof stayed on. Everything stayed complete. People fled to the church for refuge. Nobody died in that church. The same cannot be said about other places, but God took care of the church built in memory of Beth. Now, Bishop Elie Buconyori, our former student, who is currently the African bishop of our church in Burundi says the district of the Free Methodist Church where that church stands in Burundi is the strongest district in the country.

Isaiah 61:1-3

l. to r.: Len, Ed, Beth and Margi.
Then single picture is Beth, then Beth with Jim and me.
At the bottom is the picture of the memorial church

Chapter 28

Forgiveness

As I have said elsewhere, the culture is different in each country. When a girl gets married in Burundi, she leaves everything behind in her parents' home. Her groom even provides clothes for her. Her father and brothers cannot enter her home traditionally, nor can they attend her wedding. In Rwanda, it's as if the two families are joined in the wedding. In both countries, if people intermarry as many do between the Hutu and Tutsi tribes, your tribe depends on the tribe of your father. We had people from both tribes in the Free Methodist Church, not only just as members but also in the leadership of the church. The Free Methodist Church in central Africa has been exemplary in the way the two tribes care for each other in times of distress. I have tried to show that in the stories I have shared.

For the last eight years (1996-2004) of our lives in Africa, I directed and taught in the Christian Ministries Programme of the Nairobi Evangelical Graduate School of Theology (NEGST), now known as Africa International University (AIU) in Kenya. To teach the spiritual formation class, I used

Richard J. Foster's book *Celebration of Discipline.* In the chapter on The Discipline of Confession, Foster begins with the words, "At the heart of God is the desire to give and to forgive." Then in the next paragraph he says, "Love, not anger, brought Jesus to the cross."

It would seem that people are put in certain places by divine appointment to help protect others or put in certain places to be protected. I am remembering my acquaintances in Butare: women government workers and wives of businessmen. I found them more than once gathered around a radio, listening to the threats of decimating the Tutsi population . . . . I would say to them, "Don't you think you should leave? This sounds so scary to me."

They laughed and answered, "No, Butare has always been safe. No conflict has ever come here. It will be the same this time." But the women were mistaken. The conflict did come, and they were all killed. One was among those that refused to go with Ben.

Ben was a Tutsi, who was with us during our time at Kibogora Hospital mission station, and he was in the capital of Kigali when we were attempting to start new churches in the rest of Rwanda. He was a good friend of our family. He spent many days painting and varnishing to get the Kigali mission house ready for occupancy. His father was day watchman for years on the Kibogora mission station. Not much happened without his father's knowledge. His mother was a leader among the women on Kibogora hill. Both his parents were killed in the catastrophe of 1994. Ben himself was working in Kigali at that time. When the killing of 1994 started, he fled to Butare and begged his friends to go with him to Burundi. His tribe was in control at that time in Bujumbura. They refused to leave. He went alone to the border, cleared immigration and walked across to the Burundi side where he was manhandled and returned to the Rwanda side. He worked himself into the group of money-changers who are always at the borders, trying to make a profit from exchanging one country's money for another's, and walked to the next border with them. There was always a short distance of "no man's land" between countries' borders. Kind people at the Burundi border hid him till nightfall and then got a ride for him to Bujumbura. Ben was saved alone.

Ben went from Burundi to Uganda, and when the new regime came into being in Rwanda, he returned home. Ben will always be a member of his tribe, but he did what very few people in Africa ever do: he went home to Rwanda and married a woman who had been widowed in the tribal conflict. He can never forget the scars he carries because of his and his siblings' loss of their elderly parents in such a cruel way. (The parents are buried in a common grave at the entrance to Kibogora Hospital mission station. A monument stands in memory of those who died that year.) Still, Ben lives among the people who could have been his enemies but who choose to live in peace. He has forgiven, but he still has a hard time living with it. When we try to hold a neutral stand, he considers we are on the side of the other tribe.

I am remembering Pastor Silas' son Samuel. Pastor Silas and his wife were slaughtered, about the time the pastor from the other tribe was receiving Samuel to hide him. The pastor from the other tribe hid Samuel as long as he could, then, late at night, he took Samuel down to the lake and put him in a boat and shoved him away from shore. Samuel thought he would surely die because he did not know how to swim. He thought the pastor was trying to kill him by pushing him out in a boat which he did not know how to paddle. He went to sleep in the boat. When he woke up, he was far out on the lake, so he decided to try to row and rowed to safety on the other side. The important part of that story is that Samuel and that pastor who shoved him out in the boat were from differing tribes. Samuel will be forever grateful to a man of God that saved his life.

Maybe it is easier to forgive and help the opposite tribe if someone has saved you. That is what had happened to that pastor who saved Samuel 20 years before. He had been hidden under the back seat of a car and slipped across the border. The pastor had been in the process of building a new home in Bujumbura. The people stole all his building materials and he never has been able to return to his home, but he is at peace in a different country in a very fruitful ministry. He was lead pastor for 40 years in a thriving church in another country and 15 years as a hospital chaplain. Congolese women who had gone across to Bujumbura to sell their wares helped the pastor's wife dress like a Congolese market woman, walking her across the border into Congo to safety. She later joined her husband.

I am remembering Anonciate, a pastor's wife and a close friend of mine. I don't remember where her husband was at the time. I do know he survived. Anonciate was Rwandan; her husband was our student at Mweya, a Burundian. He moved to Rwanda and found and married Anonciate. Then after the 1994 hostilities, they moved back to Burundi. Anonciate was fleeing from Uvira in Congo across from Bujumbura, Burundi, with her children. Soldiers were shooting people as they fled. She held on to her children and ran in the lake, hoping the bullets would miss them and not ricochet from the water and hit them. In the night she found a house with an open door on the Congo side of the lake. She went in with her children and lay down to sleep. When they woke up in the morning, they discovered they had slept with corpses of people who had been killed without realizing it. Anonciate traveled south in Congo to the Baraka station. Several times on her way she met a man who had had his arms chopped off and had infection and a raging fever. She described her helplessness in trying to help him. After two weeks when she could not get to Tanzania, she returned to Uvira. There she found that every member of the choir in which she sang had been spared. Anonciate's question to me was "Why were we spared when so many others perished?" How do you answer that question? Only God knows.

In 1990, internal refugee camps were established in northern Rwanda; one was for Tutsis and one for Hutus. Tutsis were coming back into Rwanda from Uganda and could not find places to live. I visited those camps because of my responsibilities with International Child Care Ministries. I remember well the story of one Tutsi woman who had been living in southern Rwanda. She said she walked out of her house carrying her Bible so that people would know she was going to church. No one bothered her. However, when she got back to her house all the windows and doors were gone. She was praising God that her life had been spared.

When I heard these stories, I felt like my heart would break. It was as if the people had no country, but even then, although they had no country, no place to call home, they had an identity with God. When a person loses everything, even to the point of not being accepted in the country of his birth, he still has an inheritance that cannot be taken away from him. First Peter 1:3-5 reads: "Blessed be the God and Father of our Lord Jesus Christ, which according to his abundant mercy hath begotten us again unto a lively hope by the resurrection of Jesus Christ from the dead, to an inheritance incorruptible, and undefiled, and that fades not away, reserved in heaven for you, who are kept by the power of God through faith unto salvation ready to be revealed in the last time."

Two days after visiting the Tutsi group, I went to the Hutu refugee camp. These Hutus were refugees of 1972 from Burundi who had fled to Rwanda and had been living there ever since. This time in the early 1990's in the night the marauding Tutsis from Uganda had attacked them. The men were still up and awake in the Hutu homes. As the Tutsis came in the front of their houses, the Hutu fathers slipped out the back. The mothers handed the children out the windows to the fathers. They spent the night in the bushes and among the coffee trees. I was surprised that no women came to the appointment that day, because they were my friends from our Burundi days. When I asked why the women had not come, the men answered that the women had fled in their night clothes and had nothing decent to wear to the meeting. The refugee camp had not yet been established for them the first time I went. Hundreds of people were huddled together in a coffee warehouse. The scene was one of unbelievable hunger and need.

That morning in prayer I felt distinctly impressed that I was to read to them First Peter 1:3-9. The Word of God spoke to them better than any person's word could. Those words reveal that those who have been given new birth and a living hope have also been given an inheritance that can never perish. It was as if those verses were written especially for them. Burundi men cried. That was something I had never seen before but they were blessed with fresh hope. God met us that day in an unforgettable way.

*   *   *

Jim and I live by Philippians 4:8. "Whatever is true, noble, right, pure, lovely, admirable, excellent or praiseworthy, think about such things." During the horrible political struggles, we could do nothing for the dead, but we did our best to help, love, and comfort the living. In the wiping out of millions and with as many fleeing Rwanda in 1994, I am thankful to be able to say that International Child Care Ministries were there to help the suffering. In that year, other aid groups that had sponsored children immediately dropped their sponsorships when the families fled. Free Methodists did not do that. We were very careful not to double-sponsor any child because so many needed help. We followed them into refugee camps and tracked them down.

Another way Free Methodists helped was through transportation and rescue. We brought three plane loads of church leaders out of Tingitingi who had fled through the Ituri forest. They had walked for 250 miles. They had survived by digging up and eating a root they found in the forest. That is what kept them alive. They told us that the smell of death never left them as they walked because people would succumb along the way. Nobody could stop to bury them. They had to stay ahead of the wave of genocide.

I remember well one Free Methodist pastor who had come to Kenya on one of those planes. He came to church on Sunday morning at Karen. He asked us to pray for his wife who was very ill. They had found her brother in Nairobi and were staying with him. They had just arrived a couple days before on a plane we had sent. Sunday afternoon I found a physician, Dr. Mary Grace from Kibogora who had escaped to Nairobi, and took her to visit the wife where she lay at her brother's house. She was like a bag of bones lying on the bed, unconscious. We carried her to our car and took her to the hospital. Believe it or not, a woman physician from Rwanda was employed at that Kenyan hospital and was on duty that Sunday afternoon to receive her. I felt like shouting "Hallelujah!" The pastor's wife was ill with typhoid fever. The next day I went to visit her in the hospital and she was awake and conscious. She had been ill for days in Congo and had prayed that someone who spoke her language in Kenya would receive her. She did not know English or Swahili at that time. She said she thought she would never sleep on a mattress again or between clean sheets. When she awakened, she found herself in a clean bed. At first, she thought she had gone to heaven. She said that she had been so ill at Tingitingi. She decided if she lay on the ground she would hurt, and if she stood up and taught the women she would hurt, so she might as well teach the women. There were many in that group who fled who did not know God, and she wanted them to know the Good News. While that couple was fleeing and she was ill, she told her husband she wished she could have some meat. Her husband said he felt so bad because he could do nothing to help her, so he went and stood on the path wondering what he was going to do. Suddenly here came a man selling meat! The pastor had no idea where the man came from, but the man accepted the money he had and the pastor prepared the meat for his wife.

Another pastor went to sleep on the ground hungry. When he woke up at daybreak, there was a big papaya lying on the ground beside his head. He thought, "Is somebody trying to poison me by putting poison in this papaya by my head?" Then he thought, "I am so hungry. If I don't eat this, I will die of hunger. If it is poisoned, I will die. So I might as well eat it." He said that papaya sustained him all that day as he walked through the forest to Tingitingi. I tell you, God took care of His own.

The United Nations reported that 400,000 people fled to Tingitingi. Of those, 150,000 eventually returned to Rwanda, 50,000 died on the way, and 200,000 were massacred. When the United Nations demanded an investigation some months later, the inspectors were held off for nearly a month while the evidence was burned. The evidence that had been buried was dug up and burned, as well.

Those 400,000 fled with those of nations allied against them in hot pursuit. The rationale for pursuit was that the perpetrators of the genocide in Rwanda were hiding among the masses. This was their logic for killing the masses.

I have a copy of a Fax that I sent to our children in January, 1994, of one trip we made. I wrote, "A taxi load (small bus) was going from *(location deleted)* to *(location deleted)* along the river. Soldiers stopped the taxi and took (the opposite tribe) out and shot them. Among those killed were (people we knew). A pastor went with workers to bury the dead. He said there the corpses lay, stacked like firewood or bricks. Tears were rolling down his cheeks as he told us. He said if he had had a gun, he would have killed. He said it's really hard to love somebody that's killed your children and asked us to pray for them to be able to love their neighbors."

We were in Nigeria when the airplane carrying the presidents of Burundi and Rwanda was shot down in 1994. I went outside where Jim was talking to Mike Reynen, who was then serving in Nigeria, and gave them the news I had heard on BBC radio at 9 p.m. Jim said, "Well, our lives are forever changed." At the time, we didn't realize how true his words were. We were unable to get back into Rwanda for 10 months. The United Nations would not let us go. When we did get back, we found out the Hutu army captain, who had lived right behind us, had regularly raided our home during the nights. Our back yards joined. He threatened our guard with death if he did not tie up our dog. Our Tutsi guard was killed. Our dog eventually got out of our yard. My Tutsi assistant in ICCM found him dead beside the road having been hit by a car. He may have also starved.

When the government in control changed and Tutsis started to rule, our home became a haven for my Tutsi assistant, who was saved in a group downtown which sang the praises of God while the raid was going on in Butare. That group was not touched! Then a former Tutsi student of mine, a woman who had had both Achilles tendons slashed, and her Hutu husband stayed in our home. They were in the Swedish Pentecostal Church. Eventually they made it to Europe where she could have the needed surgery so that she could walk again. When we finally were allowed by the UN to return 10 months after the slaughter began, we found the windows of our home all broken out; the doors bashed in; filing cabinets kicked in; papers strewn; our treasures were gone. I still feel guilty for feeling sad about our loss, when others had suffered so much more. What haunts me the most was that my assistant's two children came to our house, thinking they would be safe there, but they were killed right in our yard. Their parents were saved as they sang God's praises, but were left to grieve the loss of their children. The neighbor across the street buried the children. We found an apartment in Nairobi to live in that year and spent our time doing our best to comfort the mourning.

Bonhoeffer wrote in his book *Life Together* (118) that "Anybody who lives beneath the Cross and has discerned in the Cross of Jesus the utter wickedness of all men and of his own heart will find there is no sin that can ever be alien to him. Anybody who has once been horrified by the dreadfulness of his own sin that nailed Jesus to the Cross will no longer be horrified by even the rankest sins of a brother."

Without the power of Christ in our lives enabling us to love, anyone is capable of doing horrible things. A young man trained by Christians and taught the Gospel is capable of training others to hate and to kill as long as he is paid enough and has never really yielded to the claims of the Gospel. A good Tutsi student, really a prince in demeanor, in the high school at Kibogora, was hired to take Hutu boys into the game park. He taught them to hate, to kill, to convince others to work in gangs to kill their Tutsi neighbors. They had their own radio station of propaganda used to instill fear in the Tutsis, to forecast what was coming. He succeeded. Even his own father was killed. His mother fled to the other side of Congo. He fell from favor with his leaders in crime and fled for his life. He went to his mother when he realized what he had done and died in her arms, crying and begging God's forgiveness.

Whereas we may forgive and be at peace with God and try to reconcile a situation, it may be that the other party will not receive forgiveness. A nasty situation may last a long time. We must give that to God, who judges fairly and to whom belongs retribution. We may make every effort at reconciliation, but there comes a time when Paul's phrase, "as much as lies in you," comes to an end (Romans 12:18). To keep worrying about a wrong we cannot make right is to lose our peace and, perhaps, to try to take God's prerogative. The words, "just let it go," and "drop it" must be applied many times.

Anastase Rugirangoga was a classic example of how to live. He and his family went back to Rwanda after graduating from Nairobi Evangelical Graduate School of Theology in Kenya after the cataclysmic epoch. They were there to teach and preach reconciliation. We are one body, as Paul said in Romans 12: 5, "So in Christ we who are many form one body, and each member belongs to all the others." We are not our own; we've been bought at a price. I Corinthians 6:19b, 20a.

Colossians 3:12-14 tells us how to live, no matter what happens. We always have the opportunity to follow these words, ". . . As God's chosen people, . . . clothe yourselves with compassion, kindness, humility, gentleness and patience. Bear with each other and forgive whatever grievances you may have against one another. Forgive as the Lord forgave you. And over all these virtues put on love, which binds them all together in perfect unity."

A P P E N D I X

AFRICA REVIVAL
FELLOWSHIP

A.R.F.—FULFILLING CHRIST'S CALL
TO EVANGELISM

Written by Virgil Leroy Kirkpatrick (Jim's father)
in August, 1988

Revival evangelism was born in my life when I was saved in the spring of 1919. God did a wonderful job of fulling II Corinthians 5:17 in me: "old things passed away, and all things became new." He transformed a conceited boy striving for his own glory to one earnestly striving for God's glory. I so wanted others to know the peace and well being that possessed me that I helped seventeen of my friends, some of them baseball teammates, to give their lives to Christ during the same revival meeting. During seven years at Asbury College and Theological Seminary, several of us formed gospel teams. During the school year, groups went out into the back areas of eastern Kentucky, and conducted meetings in schools, churches, hospitals and prisons. Good music and earnest, though often not very masterful preaching, strong in emphasis on the joy of a Spirit filled life kept our programs in demand. Prayer backing and God's blessing brought outstanding results. Usually two preachers and two musicians worked tent meetings sometimes sponsored by several churches. It seemed easier to see good results in tent meetings.

Dr. Eugene Erny, later president of Oriental Missionary Society; Byron Crouse, and I were in close fellowship in most of these programs. After graduating from seminary, we all went on the revival meeting trail separately. I was in Miami, Florida with Byron Crouse in a revival meeting when I received a letter from Eugene inviting me to consider joining him in an extended series of revival campaigns in Asia. Byron was eager to go with us. We purchased a 50 vy 120 foot tent that would accommodate 2,000 people, to be shipped to Korea after we had used it for summer campaigns in the USA.

From September 1929 to February 1930, we worked our way west from Baltimore, Maryland, with a full schedule of revival and missionary meetings. All offerings went for the Asian trip. We hoped to raise enough for our ship passage to Japan, Korea, and return to USA. However, offerings were so good that we bought tickets to take us around the world. Hundreds of friends from churches we had served in Pasadena and Los Angeles gave us a royal farewell early in February of 1930.

During the next eighteen months, God blessed us with one of the richest periods of revival evangelism I have experienced in twenty or more countries of Asia and the Middle East. It was natural that I went to Africa in 1932 with three main objectives: 1) evangelism, 2) church planting and 3) the training of African nationals for Christian service.

Willis R. Hotchkiss, an outstanding preacher in both Swahili and English had established the Lumbwa Industrial Mission in 1908 and planted many churches with dedicated Christian workers among the Kipsigis people during the next twenty years. He invited the National Holiness Association to take over his African mission which included Tenwek, a choice mission station located above a waterfall with enough power potential to foresee any future needs. We expected to occupy Tenwek as soon as we had mastered enough Swahili to communicate. The Africans refused permission to let us do so for over two years. However, they welcomed revival meetings and Christian workers retreats. I spent much of this time on safari at the numerous outstation churches of the African Inland Mission and Lumbwa Industrial Mission churches, and I camped many times at Tenwek. Some of these meetings were extended series of several weeks with twenty or thirty preachers of both missions. We had two services a day for the local people and several hours of Bible study classes for Christian workers. These majored on the Spirit-filled life. Most of the preachers sought the experience of entire sanctification during these meetings and their ministries became greatly enriched. Our Lord also blessed these meetings with hundreds of conversions, and several new churches were started.

During this time, we built a mission rest cottage on the sixty acre farm we had purchased from Rev. Hotchkiss. Our last months of this term in Kenya were devoted to finishing the building of this cottage and holding revival meetings among the churches in the northern half of the Kipsigis reserve. In January 1936, Faye, Marilyn, Donald, and I embarked on a freighter from Mombasa. Marilyn, eleven months old, soon became seriously ill as we sailed south. We left ship at Port Elizabeth, South Africa where she went to be with Jesus a day after her first birthday. It was a sad ending of a very wonderful first term of African service. Memories of the rich harvest of souls that God had given us during this term was a great sustaining assurance that God was with us and would use our loss to greatly enrich our ministry in the days to come.

We arrived in Kenya for our second term near the end of 1937. We were commissioned to start new work in the Congo or Ruanda-Urundi. However, funds for the new mission were lost in a bank failure during the Depression. It was almost two years before we had the means for the move to Congo, so I was again able to enjoy a period of revival evangelism in Kenya. We did make a scouting tour to Ruanda-Urundi early in 1939 and had planned to open a new field in southeast Urundi where we moved the following September.

Two prospective missionaries were added to our family, Virgil Eugene "Jim", now general superintendent of three Free Methodist conferences in central Africa, and Charles Byron "Tim," who directed Radio CORDAC in Burundi for several years and is now professor of telecommunications at Taylor University. Tim is also Co-Director of our Africa Revival Fellowship mission program.

During the next fifteen years, it was our God given privilege to start or participate in the early development of four mission stations in Urundi (later known as Burundi), with scores of outstations and thousands of Christian adherents. This was also the work of many other missionaries as the NHMS (now known as WGM) mission staff had greatly increased over the years. We also continued our revival evangelism with the National Holiness Missionary Society and other missions.

We occupied Kayero Mission in November of 1939. It was given to the National Holiness Missionary Society by the Free Methodists who had built a three room sun-dried brick residence, a temporary chapel, and had one outstation church. The Colletts who preceded us there had been forced to leave due to serious illness. Kayero continued to be our residence until we started Murore Mission in 1948. This area of 100,000 people had no Protestant churches except a small isolated area near the Ruvuvu, Burundi's largest river. A number of people had moved there due to political trouble; their preachers had followed and established seven small churches. The Church of England missionaries asked us to supervise these churches which we were glad to do, although the only way to get to most of them was to walk several miles over rugged mountain trails. The rapid development at these new stations, Murore and Murehe was due in part to the Bible classes we conducted for several years at Kayero Mission. Every day the work program terminated at 2 o'clock, and we had two hours of Bible classes four days a week. Many of the preachers from outstations in later years walked to these classes. It also provided us with Christian workers for the Kayero area expansion as well as Murehe and Murore Missions. As outstation churches developed, we had preachers from this school to lead them.

Faye and I never lived at Murehe, our second Burundi Mission, but I camped there often, set the boundaries, planted an orchard and did some preliminary building. I also conducted numerous revival meetings throughout the area and helped the African preachers start several churches. Ruth and Bill Cox were responsible for most of the early development at Murehe with the help of George Luce. Bill also started work in the Burundi refugee camps while still at Murehe and continued it from Murore Mission later. Many churches were planted in the same refugee areas of eastern Burundi. Here again Africa Revival Fellowship played a part in the growth of these churches and we are still sponsoring sixteen of them.

During these meetings with the refugees, results were outstanding. The refugees were very hungry for something to give them encouragement as they had run for their lives, many from happy prosperous homes in neighboring Rwanda, to come to a strange country. They turned to Christ by the hundreds for new life and peace.

While still at Kayero, I awakened one night and caught a clear vision of Mweya Mission much as it developed in future years, with advanced worker training institution, printing plant sufficient for the needs of all Protestant missions in Burundi and Rwanda, and a school for missionaries' children. It was to be sponsored by the Friends, Free Methodists, and World Gospel Mission in union. The vision did not include the time and place. The three missions were anxious to promote it, but it was more than three years before details of working rules and financial backing were worked out. The Free Methodists had been granted a 25 acre plot for a mission station in central Burundi but had no plans to develop it. It was ideal for the location of this union Christian workers training and publishing program.

I was appointed to Mweya in late 1949. We began work there in June of 1950. We soon had more than a hundred workmen building, procuring rock, planting timber trees and orchards, and generally developing the missions. We started Bible School in November in a renovated temporary chapel. Desks and seats were reeds tied on stakes with cross poles.

Living quarters for students consisted of several grass huts shaped like igloos, but we rapidly developed permanent quarters for them. The school program was heavy; six hours a day in school from 8 o'clock until 2 o'clock, with the students joining in the work program from 2 until 5 or 6 pm.

The next three and a half years were probably the most important of my African ministry. Spiritual tides were high at the school. On weekends students formed gospel teams and had meetings in many of the churches of Burundi. During the three month vacations each year, the students branched out into Rwanda, eastern Zaire, (formerly the Congo), and the more remote areas of Burundi. Reports of these meetings were thrilling: six hundred young people came to Christ during one of the team meetings in eastern Zaire. God wonderfully answered Faye's and my often repeated prayer, "Lord, help us to send out Spirit filled soul-winners." I also continued to participate in revival meetings and preachers' retreats during weekends and vacations.

Our first three year graduating class completed its work in the fall of 1953. Most of these students went directly into Christian service. Some had come to us from Rwanda and Zaire. Pastor training was later developed in each of these countries, but for many years standards at Mweya were higher, especially after we added a college-grade seminary to the high school-grade Bible school.

Toward the end of my third term in Africa, I often had the impression that God wanted me to launch out into full time revival evangelism, especially among the more remote churches that had very little in terms of evangelism programs. I had expected to do this with the World Gospel Mission, but when this did not work out, Africa Revival Fellowship was born.

A.R.F. began work in Africa in the spring of 1956. A group of pastors and business people in the Philadelphia area formed a board of trustees. We had good financial backing from friends who had supported me for many years. The Mweya station became our African headquarters. Due to God's blessing on many years of helping most of the missions in Rwanda, Burundi, and eastern Zaire, our schedule was soon filled for two years in advance. We had a thirty by sixty tent, good projection, amplifying, lighting, camping equipment and a 4-wheel drive Ford truck with a big transport trailer. Most of our time was spent on these gospel safaris. During the next twenty years, except for furlough time and two years teaching at Mweya, we conducted thirty to forty revival campaigns a year, each lasting six to eight days, in a dozen east and central African countries. We worked with various denominations and independent missions. We served with local African teams who organized the meetings, supplied personal workers, conducted opening services, and did some of the preaching. The programs were strenuous. The daily program included early morning prayer meeting, one or two children's meetings, a mid-day evangelistic service, one or two hours of Bible study for Christian workers, and a night meeting with either motion pictures or Bible slides built into sermons. These night meetings drew big crowds, mostly non-Christians and Catholics. We would dismiss the crowd quickly after the pictures, but urged all who had prayer burdens to stay for an after meeting. Usually hundreds would stay. We made appeals for hungry souls to come to Christ in them after meetings. I was often amazed at the numbers who came. I have not usually kept accounts of the numbers who found renewal or new life in these meetings, but did so for one ten year period. They averaged more than 5,000 a year. About a third were children, another third backslidden Christians who needed renewal or spiritual infilling, and the rest were new decisions for Christ.

These campaigns became too strenuous for me after 1977, and we concentrated our Africa Revival Fellowship energies on helping sixteen churches with thirty Christian workers in the refugee area of eastern Burundi. According to recent reports, the Lord's blessing is still upon these churches and the work is progressing well.

We praise God for His blessing upon this worthwhile ministry over the years and thank all our friends who have continued to support it with prayers and giving.

V. L. Kirkpatrick

CPSIA information can be obtained
at www.ICGtesting.com
Printed in the USA
FFHW011943050319
50891088-56293FF

9 781477 215678